PERGAMON INTERNATIONAL LIBRARY
of Science, Technology, Engineering and Social Studies
The 1000-volume original paperback library in aid of education, industrial training and the enjoyment of leisure
Publisher: Robert Maxwell, M.C.

THE STIGMA OF POVERTY

A Critique of Poverty Theories and Policies

OTHER PERGAMON TITLES OF INTEREST

Evans & Claiborn—*Mental Health Issues and the Urban Poor*
Monahan—*Community Mental Health in the Criminal Justice System*
Morrice—*Crisis Intervention—Studies in Community Care*
Nietzel et al—*Behavioral Approaches to Community Psychology*
Hall—*Black Separatism and Social Reality*
Halpern—*Survival—Black/White*

THE STIGMA OF POVERTY

A Critique of Poverty Theories and Policies

by

Chaim I. Waxman
Rutgers University

Pergamon Press

New York/Toronto/Oxford/Sydney/Frankfurt/Paris

Pergamon Press Offices:

U.S.A.	Pergamon Press Inc., Maxwell House, Fairview Park, Elmsford, New York 10523, U.S.A.
U.K.	Pergamon Press Ltd. Headington Hill Hall, Oxford OX3, OBW, England
CANADA	Pergamon of Canada, Ltd., 207 Queen's Quay West, Toronto 1, Canada
AUSTRALIA	Pergamon Press (Aust) Pty. Ltd., 19a Boundary Street, Rushcutters Bay, N.S.W. 2011, Australia
FRANCE	Pergamon Press SARL, 24 rue des Ecoles, 75240 Paris, Cedex 05, France
WEST GERMANY	Pergamon Press GmbH, 6242 Kronberg/Taunus, Frankfurt-am-Main, West Germany

---

Library of Congress Cataloging in Publication Data
Waxman, Chaim Isaac.
The stigma of poverty.

Bibliography: p.
Includes index.
1. Poor—United States. 2. Economic assistance, Domestic—United States. 3. Poverty. I. Title.
HC110.P6W32 1977 301.44'1 77-5760
ISBN 0-08-021800-8
ISBN 0-08-021798-2 pbk.

Printed in the United States of America

In Memory of

My Brother

David B. Waxman ז״ל

CONTENTS

PREFACE

The subject of poverty—no longer the top priority of government agencies that deal with social policy and no longer high on the lists of best-seller books—cannot be wished away or banished by "benign neglect." As public attitudes towards the poor become decreasingly benevolent, the problems of poverty for the poor grow more intolerable.

The very fact that poverty is no longer in the limelight offers us the opportunity to analyze it more carefully than was possible a decade ago. Daniel Patrick Moynihan has argued that one of the major defects of the "war on poverty" was that it was too hastily conceived. The enthusiasm, idealism, and zeal contributed to "maximum feasible misunderstanding." Moreover, as shall be seen in this study, fierce competition for project funding led to bitter conflicts which often only exacerbated the problem by distorting our understanding of it.

In the present climate, on the other hand, it is possible for cooler heads to prevail. Though no longer a topic for those on the lecture circuit, poverty remains a major subject of study in undergraduate and graduate departments of sociology, urban affairs, and social work. Hopefully, those who will be in positions to influence future social policy will have had good exposure to one or a number of these departments. Along this line, this study concludes with a number of modest proposals for social policy. The limited nature of these derives not from any false pretenses of humility, but from the firm conviction that there are no panaceas. We subscribe to the wisdom of Solomon: that it is better not to promise than to promise and not live up to that promise. If this work contributes in some small way to a clearer understanding of and/or to effective social policies for dealing with poverty and related problems, the many years of time and effort which went into it will have been more than compensated for.

My own interest and involvement with the subject derive from the moral and value systems instilled in me by my parents, my work experience with the New York City Department of Welfare and the Yonkers Community Action, Inc., course work and a doctoral dissertation at The New School for Social Research, and my years of teaching at Central Connecticut State College, Brooklyn College, The New School for Social Research, and Rutgers University. In addition to my many students, I wish to thank Professors Franklin J. Watson, Jack Lucas, Ronald Fernandez, Deborah I. Offenbacher, Seymour Martin Lipset, E. V. Walter, Emile Oestereicher, Stanford Lyman, and David Muchnick, who have read and criticized various drafts of this book. Final responsibility is, of course, my own. Mrs. Sylvia M. Halpern, Chief Manuscript Editor for Pergamon Press, has my gratitude for both the professional and personal attention which she gave to the book. And, last being the most precious, I acknowledge that I can never sufficiently repay my wife, Chava, and our children, Ari, Shani, and Dani, for their understanding and encouragement.

C.I.W.

ACKNOWLEDGEMENTS

I am indebted to the following authors and publishers for their kind permission to quote from copyrighted material:

Urie Bronfenbrenner. "Socialization and Social Class Through Time and Space." In Eleanor E. Maccoby, Theodore H. Newcomb and Eugene L. Hartley (Eds.), *Readings in Social Psychology.* Third Edition. © Holt, Rinehart and Winston, 1968.

Kenneth B. Clark. *Dark Ghetto.* © Harper & Row, Inc. 1965.

Albert K. Cohen. *Delinquent Boys.* © The Free Press, 1955.

Albert K. Cohen and James F. Short, Jr. "Research in Delinquent Subcultures." *Journal of Social Issues,* 1958, Vol. XIV, pp. 20-37. © The Society for the Psychological Study of Social Issues.

Lewis A. Coser, "Unanticipated Conservative Consequences of Liberal Theorizing." *Social Problems,* 1968-69. Vol. 16, pp. 263-272. © Society for the Study of Social Problems.

Karl de Schweinitz. *England's Road to Social Security.* © A. S. Barnes, 1961.

Lloyd A. Free and Hadley Cantril. *The Political Beliefs of Americans: A Study of Public Opinion.* © Rutgers University Press, 1967.

Hans Gerth and C. Wright Mills. *Character and Social Structure.* © Harcourt, Brace and World, 1953.

Erving Goffman. *Stigma: Notes on the Management of Spoiled Identity.* © Prentice Hall, 1963.

Marvin Harris. *The Nature of Cultural Things.* © Random House, 1964.

August B. Hollinghead and F. C. Redlich. *Social Class and Mental Illness.* © John Wiley and Sons, 1958.

John J. Honigmann. "Middle Class Values and Cross-Cultural Understanding." In Joseph C. Finney (Ed.), *Culture Change, Mental Health, and Poverty.* © University of Kentucky Press, 1969.

J. McVicker Hunt. *The Challenge of Incompetence and Poverty: Papers on the Role of Early Education.* © University of Illinois Press, 1969.

Rodger Hurley. *Poverty and Mental Retardation: A Causal Relationship.* © Random House, 1969.

Herbert H. Hyman. "The Value Systems of Different Classes." In Rheinhard Bendix and Seymour Martin Lipset (Eds.), *Class, Status and Power.* © The Free Press, 1953.

W. K. Jordan. *Philanthropy in England, 1480-1660.* © Russell Sage Foundation, 1959.

Alfred L. Kroeber. *Anthropology,* Revised Edition. © Harcourt, Brace and World, 1948.

Eleanor Leacock. "Distortions of Working-Class Reality in American Social Science." *Science and Society,* 1967, Vol. XXXI, pp. 1-20. © *Science and Society.*

George Lenski. *Power and Privilege.* © McGraw-Hill Book Co., 1966.

Oscar Lewis. *Five Families.* © Basic Books, 1959.

Oscar Lewis. *La Vida.* © Random House, 1966.

Elliot Liebow. *Talley's Corner.* © Little, Brown, 1967.

Ralph Linton. *The Study of Man.* © Appleton-Century, 1936.

David Matza. *Delinquency and Drift.* © John Wiley and Sons, 1964.

David Matza. "Poverty and Disrepute." In Robert K. Merton and Robert A. Nisbet (Eds.), *Contemporary Social Problems,* Second Edition. © Harcourt, Brace and World, 1966.

Kurt B. Mayer and Walter Buckley. *Class and Society,* Third Edition. © Random House, 1970.

Robert K. Merton. "Social Structure and Anomie." *American Sociological Review.* 1938, Vol. 3, pp. 672-682. © American Sociological Association.

S. M. Miller and Pamela Roby. *The Future of Inequality.* © Basic Books, 1970.

Walter B. Miller. "Lower Class Culture as a Generating Milieu of Gang Delinquency." *Journal of Social Issues,* 1958, Vol. XIV, pp. 5-19. © The Society for the Psychological Study of Social Issues.

Daniel P. Moynihan. *The Politics of a Guaranteed Income.* © Random House, 1973.

Robert E. Park and Ernest W. Burgess. *The City.* © University of Chicago Press, 1925.

Hyman Rodman. "The Lower Class Value Stretch." *Social Forces,* 1963, Vol. 42, pp. 205-215. © *Social Forces.*

W. G. Runciman. *Relative Deprivation and Social Justice.* © University of California Press.

Leo Srole, et. al. *Mental Health in the Metropolis: The Midtown Manhattan Study.* McGraw-Hill Book Co. © Leo Srole, 1962.

William Graham Sumner. *Folkways.* Ginn and Co., 1940. © William Graham Sumner 1906.

Gerald D. Suttles. *The Social Order of the Slum.* © University of Chicago Press, 1968.

Frederick M. Thrasher. *The Gang.* Abridged Edition. © University of Chicago Press, 1963.

Joseph Townsend. *A Dissertation on the Poor Laws.* University of California Press, 1971. © Regents of the University of California.

Sydney Webb and Beatrice Webb. *English Poor Law History, Part I, The Old Poor Law.* © Frank Cass & Co., Ltd., 1963.

Kathleen Woodroofe. *From Charity to Social Work.* © University of Toronto Press and Routledge & Kegan Paul, Ltd., 1966.

INTRODUCTION

There are among American sociologists and policy makers two major conceptualizations and explanations of poverty,[1] one known as the cultural perspective and the other as the situational perspective. It is the objective of this study to examine both the cultural and situational explanations, to demonstrate the ideological implications of both, and to suggest a new perspective which will be termed the relational perspective. Our intention is not to examine the causal nexus of all three models and the allegedly unique behavior patterns and value patterns of poor people. Rather, we suggest that the relational perspective would eliminate this area of debate insofar as social policy is concerned, and would permit new directions in policy which would alleviate the implications of the stigma.

Because the argument between the culturalists and the situationalists is very complex and protracted, it must be immediately pointed out that within each of these positions as they shall be critically analyzed herein, there will inevitably be issues upon which not all those whom we designate as culturalists agree. Likewise, not all the situationalists are in agreement on all issues. These disagreements should not be of major concern for the purposes of this study since they do not detract from their basic commonality of perspective.

Chapter 1 will examine the cultural perspective, according to which the lower class is seen as manifesting patterns of behavior and values which are characteristically different from those of the dominant society and culture. Furthermore, according to the culturalists, these unique patterns of behavior and values are transmitted intergenerationally through socialization and have become the subcultural *determinants* of the lower socioeconomic status of the poor.

---

[1] The criteria used in the determination of poverty and who the poor are differ, depending in part upon whether one is viewing poverty from the framework of an economist or that of a sociologist. Economists typically view the question primarily in terms of income, and they define the poor as those whose income is below minimum subsistence or minimum decent subsistence level. Since terms such as "minimum," "decent," and "subsistence" are relative, we find that even among economists there are wide variations in the determination of a poverty level. For example, during the period 1957-1960, more than a half dozen works were published concerning the extent of poverty in the United States, and the figures in these studies varied widely, depending, in part, upon the income level which was used as the poverty line (cf. Ornati, 1966, pp. 27-33).

To demonstrate and examine the cultural perspective as it pertains to the patterns of behavior and values of the poor, four variables have been selected: crime, mental illness, education, and family life. The variables selected for correlation with poverty are by no means to be taken as exclusive. There are many other patterns which may be associated with being poor/non-poor. The variables with which we deal—crime, mental illness, education, and family life—have been selected for several reasons.

Sociologists, on the other hand, have not typically viewed the question of poverty and the poor solely in terms of income. While in the past several years sociologists such as Peter Townsend, S. M. Miller, and Martin Rein have been drawn to the question of the poverty line, sociologists have taken the determination of poverty as their point of embarkation. What the precise income level is in the determination of poverty has not been the question, so much as is the matter of the effects of that determination. Most sociologists have viewed poverty within the framework of social problems and have concerned themselves with the causes and effects of poverty, primarily by studying those who have been designated as poor. Others have argued that the sociological study of poverty and the poor must also encompass the study of those who make the determination of poverty (cf. Gans, 1970, pp. 146-164; Offenbacher, 1968, p. 44).

The fact that the criteria used in the determination of poverty are not uniformly agreed upon by economists and, moreover, have until recently rarely been of major concern to sociologists, presents us with a number of important problems in examining sociological perspectives of poverty. One serious problem is that it is very often difficult to ascertain whether the sociologists are referring to the same population. Are "the poor" discussed by one the same as "the poor" discussed by another? What of "the lower class," "the working class"? One is forced to examine the context of the discussion and determine from that context whether or not the various studies are referring to, more or less, the same population. For the sociologist, this determination rests upon the understanding that he or she is not actually defining the poverty level or the size of the poor population; that has already been done by others—economists, policy makers, etc.

A second related difficulty with an examination of poverty and the poor is that the very term "the poor" often obfuscates the fact that there are often different types of poverty and poor, even within the same society at the same time. Thus, S. M. Miller has argued for clearer distinction and differentiation of sub-units which comprise the lower classes within American Society (Miller, 1964, pp. 1-22, reprinted in Riessman, Cohen, Pearl, 1964, pp. 139-154). The various types of poor and the differential stigma of poverty will be discussed in a later chapter. For the present, we would argue for the use of the broader category of "the poor," since we are dealing with the works of sociologists who have used this broader category. Moreover, it is true that not all those in the lower class are as poor or deprived as are the very poor, and thus "lower class" may not be synonymous with "poor"; however, all of the poor are certainly in the lower class. Therefore, when patterns of behavior and values of the lower class are shown to be different from those of the middle class, it may safely be assumed that these would apply, perhaps even more so, to the poor. But this certainly does not mean that they would apply to *all* of the poor, nor even to all persons in the lower class. As Joseph A. Kahl (1957) points out:

> These ideal-type classes are helpful abstractions, but cannot be used without practical judgment; they will help us order our thinking about the complexities of social reality, although they may encourage us to assume falsely that a community can be neatly divided with each family tagged and placed in its niche. (p. 216)

Certainly many cannot, and the extent to which there is internal variation within the lower class and different types of poor with different types of stigma will become important when we discuss social policy considerations.

First of all, they have been selected because they fall into the category of social problems and our entire work considers the subject of poverty within the context of social problems. Secondly, there is a more extensive body of literature which deals with these patterns than with others. Moreover, it is with these patterns that the explanations can be most clearly shown to flow from either a cultural or situational perspective. Thirdly, and this relates back to the first reason, many of the action programs designed to alleviate or eradicate poverty relate to these patterns. Since one of our objectives is to analyze the theoretical framework of these programs and to demonstrate their weaknesses, we have selected these four variables.

Finally, since our analysis focuses upon the stigma of poverty and the moral judgments that are made of the poor, we have selected variables that are commonly associated with the moral judgments concerning the poor; the belief that the poor have no morality (i.e., they steal, mug, are loose sexually), are lazy, don't want to get an education and improve themselves, and are a bunch of "sickies," has not disappeared from the American scene. It began in Europe close to a thousand years ago and persists in America to this day. The patterns of behavior of the poor in these four areas are crucial to the analysis of the stigma of poverty. The cultural and situational perspectives take these four traits as characteristic of the poor and, as such, present an ideological position of the poor in that they ignore the relationship between the poor and the non-poor.

Chapter 1 will demonstrate that with each of the variables the culturalists establish the unique patterns of the lower class and explain these patterns as being internally or subculturally derived. With respect to crime and delinquency in the lower class, the cultural approach finds its clearest expression in the writing of Walter B. Miller, who states explicitly that lower class gang delinquency is a direct product of lower class culture, which has its unique values, or "focal concerns," and traditions that are many centuries old.

After documenting the evidence which indicates that the lower class has a significantly higher rate of schizophrenia than the higher classes, we assert that it is those who explain this in accordance with the "labeling approach," such as John J. Honigmann and others, who are basically culturalists. By virtue of their argument that it is middle class psychiatrists who label the behavior of persons in the lower class as symptomatic of mental disorder because they are unfamiliar with the norms of behavior in the lower class, these critics are, in effect, arguing that there is a lower class culture that is essentially different from that of the middle class. Thus, even though they deny that this lower class culture is actually pathological, they do agree that it is unique, different.

Turning to education and the lower class, the literature shows the problems of lower class children in school, and the cultural explanations of Allison Davis, Arnold W. Green, Jackson Toby, and Basil Bernstein are presented. While the specifics of their explanations differ, it is shown that each of their explanations is based upon a cultural perspective of poverty and the poor.

Finally, in the area of family life, we find Lee Rainwater explaining the higher birthrate in the lower class from a definitely cultural perspective.

Having presented the cultural perspective of poverty, the remainder of this chapter discusses the policy implications which derive from this definition of the problem, since in the United States poverty has been judged to be a social problem.[2] It will be shown that such approaches as social casework, counseling and guidance, compensatory education, and cultural enrichment programs derive from the cultural perspective.

Chapter 2 will examine the situational perspective, according to which the behavior patterns of the poor are not seen as pathologies nor are they seen as being internally derived as the products of a unique value system. Rather, the behavior patterns of the poor are seen as normal results of situations where the dominant social structure is unfavorably disposed toward and restricts the options of the lower class. It is precisely because the poor do share in the dominant values of the social and cultural system that they turn to behavior which becomes labeled as deviant and pathological. The basic problem is not one of internally determining cultural values but rather of externally determining situational factors caused by the disproportionately restrictive social structure. As with the cultural perspective, we find that this perception of poverty and the poor underlies many of the explanations of the behavior patterns of the poor with reference to the four variables selected.

Insofar as the crime rate of the lower class is concerned, one of the most acclaimed explanations is that of Robert K. Merton, who attributed it to the social structure which limits opportunity, while at the same time the cultural system espouses an ideology of success that is attainable by all. After demonstrating the limitations of Merton's theory, the chapter proceeds to examine the cultural transmission approach of Frederick Thrasher, and the more recent delinquent subculture approaches of Albert Cohen, Richard A. Cloward, and Lloyd Ohlin. Finally, the reformu-

---

[2] One attempt at an organization of the theory and research in order to explore the social policy implications may be found in an article by Martin Rein, "Social Science and the Elimination of Poverty" (1967, reprinted in Rein, 1970, Chapter 20, pp. 417-445). Rein's discussion, which is primarily policy-oriented, is organized around the perspectives of "resource allocation, social and personal theory, and institutional performance." Since our discussion is more theory-oriented, the cultural and situational perspectives are the bases for our organization.

lation of this approach by David Matza is reviewed. From all of these, which are in essence the major explanations of lower class crime and delinquency, we derive a view of the lower class adhering to the dominant value system of the society but being subjected to social structural constraints and seeking to adapt as best they can to this overbearing situation. The theorists of situational adaptation are, thus, structuralists, in contrast with Walter B. Miller, who is clearly a culturalist.

A number of situational explanations of the higher rate of schizophrenia among the poor are then reviewed. John A. Clausen and Melvin Kohn suggest size of the city as a factor. This is then related to the finding of John B. Calhoun in his study of the effects of population density upon the behavior of domesticated rats. Finally, the work of Abram Hoffer in treating schizophrenics with injections of niacin is introduced and related to that of Clausen, Kohn, and Calhoun. Before turning to the next variable, the "drift hypothesis" is briefly examined.

With respect to the educational problems of the poor, the views of Kenneth Clark and Estelle Fuchs are stated and are shown to highlight the basic disagreements between the culturalists and the situationalists.

Finally, as to the matter of the birthrate of the poor, the findings of Frederick Jaffe and Steven Polgar indicate the gap between their situational explanation and the cultural explanation of Lee Rainwater.

As was done in the first chapter with the cultural perspective, this chapter concludes with an examination of the policy implications which derive from the situational perspective. Since this perspective defines the problem as lying in the social structure, the "solutions" or programs suggested aim at either changing the social structure per se, or, at least, changing the position of the poor within the social structure through community action programs, with the poor in a position to control those programs that affect their lives. Various manifestations of these types of programs will be explored.

Chapter 3 will subject both the cultural and situational perspectives to extensive critical analysis. The concept "subculture," which is basic to Oscar Lewis, the most widely known of the culturalists, and to Charles A. Valentine and other situationalists, will be scrutinized in detail, and the fallacies inherent in both perspectives will be revealed.

Chapter 4 will develop the relational perspective of poverty, which rests upon an understanding of the position of the poor within the social structure, the attitudes and actions of the non-poor toward the poor, and the effects of these upon the poor themselves. One of the few writers on the subject to recognize the untenability of both the cultural and situational perspectives is Herbert J. Gans. Gans suggests, as will be argued at some length, the unacceptability of "the tendency to see the behavior pattern as resistant to change, as persisting simply because it is culture, even though there is no real evidence for this view" (1970, p. 153). We shall put the argument more strongly and show that, on the contrary, the evidence clearly indicates that this is a false conception of culture. Also, Gans is one of the few writers on the subject to call for a "dynamic perspective" which takes cognizance of the norms, values, and aspirations of the poor, and relates them to the interaction of the poor with the non-poor. It will be argued that poverty in the United States is a stigma with similar implications as the stigma discussed by Erving Goffman. The extent of this stigma of poverty will be shown through a review of government social welfare, beginning with the first Poor Laws in England in the mid-14th century and extending to the present welfare policies in the United States. The reactions of stigmatized persons are then discussed. Goffman suggests three strategies which stigmatized individuals might adopt in order to cope with the situations of stigma. It is argued in this volume that there are also collectively derived techniques which groups may adopt to cope with their collective stigma. This is shown to be the case with some minority subcultures, which develop independent cultural systems that allow them to reject the stigmatizing dominant value system. But this is not a realistic option for the heterogeneous poor. After examining the relationship between values and social structure, it will be shown that the "culture of poverty" is not an independent subculture, but rather a dependent one; it is a subculture that develops and persists along with the stigma of poverty as part of a vicious circle. Thus, the culture of poverty is neither solely internal, as the culturalists argue, nor solely external, as the situationalists argue, for it has both internal and external sources; it is relational, a dependent subculture.

The concluding chapter begins by exploring the possibilities for breaking the cycle which results from the stigma of poverty. Alternatives on two levels, absolute and relative, are analyzed with reference to changing values and with reference to changing the social structure. The previously reviewed programs and policies deriving from the cultural perspective and those deriving from the situational perspective are subjected to critical analysis. A number of problems, in addition to their erroneous theoretical foundations, are discussed. A flaw common to all these policies and programs will be found to be their isolating effect upon the poor, thus contributing to, rather than alleviating, the stigma of poverty. The major conclusion insofar as social policy is concerned will be that effective policy must attempt to integrate the poor into the society, and a number of suggestions along these lines will be discussed. Recognizing the many pitfalls of social planning, a number of which are discussed, the conclusion stops short of boldly formulating "solutions" and "panaceas." Rather, the objective of this analysis is to indicate the direction toward which policy must proceed in the hope of alleviating, if not eradicating, the stigma of poverty.

Chapter 1

THE CULTURAL PERSPECTIVE

Since the 1960s it has been fashionable to speak of a "culture of poverty" in the United States. This term, coined by Oscar Lewis and popularized by Michael Harrington, draws from one of the two major sociological conceptualizations and explanations of poverty in American society. It refers to the lives of the poor, or at least many of the urban poor, in the United States who are seen as being different from the non-poor not only economically but in many other respects as well. Their being different, or deviant, with respect to a whole set of patterns of behavior, it is suggested, sets them apart basically from the rest of the society. According to the cultural perspective on poverty, the lower class is seen as manifesting patterns of behavior and values which are characteristically different from those of the dominant society and culture. Moreover, according to the culturalists, these unique patterns of behavior and values are transmitted intergenerationally through socialization and have become the subcultural *determinants* of the lower socioeconomic status of the poor.

To demonstrate and examine the cultural perspective as it pertains to the patterns of behavior and values of the poor, four variables have been selected: crime, mental illness, education, and family life. As stated in the Introduction, these variables have been selected because of the extensive literature available and because they are frequently referred to in support of moral judgments about the poor. This chapter will demonstrate that with each of these variables, the culturalists establish the unique patterns of the lower class and explain these patterns as being internally, or subculturally, derived.

With each of the variables to be discussed, the unique patterns of the poor concerning that variable will first be established, and the cultural explanation will immediately follow. It should be clear that our analysis is not concerned with the causal relationship between the cultural model and each of the variables, but with the ideological view of the poor implicit in this model, which not only supports the stigmatization of the poor but also carries with it certain assumptions for social policy.

CRIME

Whereas, as shall be seen in this chapter and the next, the explanations vary considerably, there is general agreement among criminologists, law enforcement officials, politicians, and the general public that there is a correlation between crime and social class—specifically, that crime is significantly more frequent in the lower class in the United States. In many cases the correlation is simply posited as self-evident, while a number of studies support it on the basis of official police, court, and FBI records.

Unquestionably, the mere fact that official records clearly indicate that crime is more frequent in the lower class cannot be taken as conclusive proof, for there have beeen severe criticisms of the official data. As early as 1940, Edwin H. Sutherland wrote an article in the *American Sociological Review*, arguing for the unreliability of the official records because they ignore a whole area of crime, "white-collar crime," because the perpetrators of this type of crime are able, for various reasons, to escape arrest and prosecution. Sutherland later elaborated upon his discussion of white-collar crime in a book by that title, published in 1949.

In recent years, one of the major official sources of data concerning crime in the United States has come under almost unanimous attack by criminologists and sociologists—namely, the FBI's "Uniform Crime Reports."[3]

And yet, despite the almost unanimous criticism of the official statistics, most criminologists accept the trend, if not to the degree, indicated by those statistics. Donald R. Cressey (1966) puts it this way:

> The reliability of the official statistics on the socioeconomic class backgrounds of criminals has been questioned even more severely than have the statistics on variables like age, race, and area of residence.
>
> ...However, the statistics on ordinary crime so consistently show an over-representation of lower class persons that it is reasonable to assume that there is a real difference between the behavior of the members of this class and the members of other social classes, so far as criminality is concerned. (p. 157)

It is this assumption that underlies almost all of American criminological theory.

Among all of the explanations of the higher rate of criminality, and especially juvenile delinquency, in the lower class, that of Walter B. Miller

---

[3] See Green, 1975; *New York Times*, 1965, 1968a, 1968b; Robison, 1966; *Time*, 1966; Wolfgang, 1963. In the *Time* article, Sophia M. Robison is quoted as saying that the FBI summaries are "not worth the paper they're printed on."

(1958) certainly must rank as one of the most purely cultural. Gang delinquency in the lower class, he argues, is a direct product of "lower class culture" itself. As he states it, "there is a substantial segment of present-day American society whose way of life, values, and characteristic patterns of behavior are the product of a distinctive cultural system which may be termed 'lower class' " (p. 6). Preferring the term "focal concerns" instead of "values," he maintains that the patterning of focal concerns in the lower class "differs significantly...from that of American middle class culture" (p. 7). Concentrating on six focal concerns and the "perceived alternatives," specifically trouble, toughness, smartness, excitement, fate, and autonomy, he maintains that the lower class defines and values these differently than does the middle class; thus, status in the lower class is defined differently than it is in the middle class. For example, since "smartness" in the lower class is not defined in terms of scholastic achievement, as it is in the middle class, but rather "involves the capacity to outsmart, outfox, outwit, dupe, 'take,' 'con' another or others, and the concomitant capacity to avoid being outwitted" (p. 9), then in the lower class "the status-conferring potential of 'smartness' in the sense of scholastic achievement generally ranges from negligible to negative" (p. 15). Or, for example, lower class concerns over "toughness"—physical prowess, "masculinity," and bravery, Miller finds rooted in, or at least "probably related to the fact that a significant proportion of lower class males are reared in a predominantly female household, and lack a consistently present male figure with whom to identify and from whom to learn essential components of a 'male' role" (p. 9).

Because of "the prevalence of a stabilized type of lower class child-rearing unit—the 'female-based' household," the typical relation unit in the lower class is the "one-sex peer unit" (p. 14), rather than the "two-parent family unit" which is characteristic of middle and upper classes in American society. As a result, lower class males need to be part of stable and solitary peer units; thus, "the adolescent street corner group variant represents the adolescent variant of this lower class structural form" (p. 14) and its focal concerns "are those of the general cultural milieu in which it functions" (p. 15). The street corner group attracts new members because of their desire to belong and their desire for status, which means conforming to the focal concerns. Contrary to a number of other theorists, especially Albert K. Cohen (whose work will be discussed in the next chapter), Miller maintains that the prime motivating factor for gang delinquency is not its violation of middle class norms. On the contrary, he argues, "it is a by-product of action primarily oriented to the lower class system. The standards of lower class culture cannot be seen as a reverse function of middle class culture...; *lower class culture is a distinctive tradition many centuries old with an integrity of its own*" (p. 19, emphasis added).

Miller's explanation of lower class gang delinquency clearly meets all the criteria of the culturalists; he posits a lower class culture with unique values ("focal concerns") which, in turn, determine the unique patterns of behavior of those members of the lower class.

MENTAL ILLNESS

There is a wide range of evidence indicating a positive correlation between poverty and mental illness, specifically schizophrenia. Studies of the socioeconomic distribution of schizophrenia date back to the beginning of this century. The best known among the early studies is that of Robert E. L. Faris and H. Warren Dunham, *Mental Disorders in Urban Areas* (1939).[4] We shall concentrate upon the more recent studies.

In 1958, August B. Hollingshead and F. C. Redlich published the results of their study of a five percent sample of all households in New Haven, Connecticut. The sample was stratified into five social classes, based on an index involving occupation, education, and area of residence. They found an inverse relationship between social class and schizophrenia, as shown in the following table:

Table 1.1 ***Incidence, re-entry, continuous, and prevalence rates per 100,000 for the schizophrenics—by class (age and sex adjusted)***

	Type of Rate per 100,000			
Class	Incidence	Re-entry	Continuous	Prevalence
I-II	6	14	97	111
III	8	20	148	168
IV	10	21	269	300
V	20	46	729	895
$x^2 =$	8.50	13.46	355.62	452.68
df	3	3	3	3
p	<.05	<.01	<.001	<001

Source: August B. Hollingshead and F. C. Redlich, *Social Class and Mental Illness.* New York: John Wiley & Sons, 1958, p. 236. Reprinted by permission.

Their findings support their two main hypotheses—that the prevalence of treated mental illness is related to the individual's social class, and that the type of illness diagnosed is related to the class structure.

S. M. Miller and Elliott G. Mishler (1964) have cautioned that the Hollingshead and Redlich data refer only to treated illness, not the incidence of illness. "The relation between treated and total illnesses in different social classes is not known and the total rates cannot be assumed to be a standard coefficient of the treated rates" (p. 29). Furthermore, their

[4] Reviews of the literature can be found in Mishler and Scotch (1965) and Roman and Trice (1967).

review of the data indicates that there is not a consistent inverse relationship between social class and mental illness, but rather a consistent difference between Class V, the lowest class, and all other classes. Their major finding, they say, is "the consistent differences between Class V and the other classes, with the differences that exist among the latter not clearly and consistently patterned in a hierarchal fashion." (p. 28).

H. Warren Dunham (1965) in an "intensive" study of two "subcommunities" in the city of Detroit, found results which correspond with the Miller and Mishler recomputation of the Hollingshead and Redlich data: "The only significant differences in the class rates for schizophrenia are found when the Class V rate is compared with the rates of the other classes" (p. 182). Insofar as Class V is concerned, he found that "in all diagnostic groups—as well as in the total cases for both subcommunities—the rates are highest in Class V" (p. 178).

The "Midtown Manhattan Study" (Srole, Langner, Michael, Kirkpatrick, Opler, & Rennie, 1962) found the relationship between social class and mental illness to be an inverse one. "In the Midtown sample of age 20 to 59 adults the over-all prevalence of mental morbidity is inversely related to the independent variable of socioeconomic status and related even more closely in this direction to the reciprocal variable of adults' present (own) SES" (p. 240). When broken down in terms of facilities used, the following shows the distribution:

Table 1.2 *Treatment census (age inclusive), prevalence rates (per 100,000 corresponding population) of midtown patients in own-SES strata by treatment site*

Treatment site	Own SES (housing indicator)		
	Upper	Middle	Lower
Hospitals:			
Public	98	383	646
Private	104	39	18
Combined in-patients	202	422	664
Clinics	61	160	218
Office therapists*	1,440	596	178
Combined out-patients	1,501	756	396
Total Patients rate	1,703	1,178	1,060
N = No. of patients§	(575)	(604)	(934)

*These rates are uncorrected for the unreported patients of noncooperating office therapists. They are corrected for patients reported with addresses lacking or verifiably false.

Source: Srole, L., Langner, T. S., Michael, S. T., Kirkpatrick, P., Opler, M. K., Rennie, T. A. C. *Mental Health in the Metropolis*, New York. McGraw-Hill Book Company, 1962, p. 241. Reprinted by permission.

The discrepancy between the Midtown data and the New Haven data may be the result of differences in variables used in the determination of social class, or it may be the result of the Midtown study's consideration of office therapists, which the New Haven study failed to consider. In any case, we again find mental illness concentrated in the lower class.

R. Jay Turner and Morton O. Wagenfeld (1967), in a study drawn from the psychiatric case register of Monroe County, New York, which records about 95% of the psychiatric contacts in the County, be they diagnostic or treatment, inpatient or outpatient, public or private, found further evidence to conclude that "analysis of the patients' occupations supported the typical finding of a disproportionate number of schizophrenics in the lowest occupational category." Furthermore, "it was determined that the fathers of the patients were also overrepresented at the lowest prestige level" (p. 113).

In sum, the evidence available from a variety of sources strongly indicates that there is an inverse relationship (even if not consistently so) between social class and schizophrenia. Most importantly, for the purposes of this study, the data seem to confirm the positive correlation between poverty and the schizophrenic form of mental illness.

When we analyze the explanations offered for the correlation between poverty and schizophrenia, an interesting and ironic situation emerges. Just as Sutherland dismissed the data showing a correlation between crime and poverty on the grounds that they were the product of biased labeling, so there are those who dismiss the data concerning schizophrenia and poverty on the grounds that they are a product of biased labeling. However, whereas Sutherland was anything but a culturalist, those rejecting the data on schizophrenia and crime are, at least implicit culturalists. Specifically, there are those who question the validity of the data on the relationship between poverty and mental illness, asserting that because of psychiatrists' class-biased expectations of "normal" behavior, they are more likely to judge certain lower class behavior as symptomatic of mental disorder. This criticism is implicit in the writings of Thomas S. Szasz. In a recent essay, for example, he writes:

> Renaming and reclassification play a fundamental role in the development, the theory, and the practice of psychiatry. Social deviance, renamed as "mental illness," became the subject matter of psychiatry; social outcasts and other incompetent, troubled, oppressed, and persecuted individuals, renamed "neurotics" and "psychotics" became the "patients" who psychiatric "physicians" were expected to "treat"; and the doctors who assumed the task of verbally or physically controlling troublesome individuals, renamed "psychiatrists," became the scientifically accredited experts in the diagnosis and treatment of "mental disease." Nearly all of this is humbug. (1970, p. 67)

Erving Goffman makes the point more explicitly when he writes: "Like everyone else, the psychiatrist is apt to interpret some conduct as improper merely because he is not familiar with the involvement idiom and the involvement rulings of *the culture of the group from which the patient comes*" (1963, p. 233, emphasis added).

The culturalist will, in line with Szasz and Goffman, therefore explain the high rate of schizophrenia in the lower class as being the result of the middle class psychiatrists' *labeling* of behavior which is perfectly normal in lower class culture, as "sick," because it is not "normal" in middle class culture. Their criticism of the data is predicated upon the notion that lower class culture is distinct from middle class culture, both of which are composed of their own unique patterns of behavior, standards, and values. Thus, John J. Honigmann (1970) in a paper questioning the findings of the Midtown study and others, asks

> if those standards are not ethnocentrically contaminated by the evaluator's own class-bound values to such a degree that those values block him from getting a fuller, truer view of the people whom he is judging. When psychiatrists include their own class-bound values in evaluating personality disorder, people who show strain by acting out or falling to pieces emotionally or cognitively, as lower class people predominantly do, are judged as worse off than people who feel unworthy or who constantly visit the doctor with difficult stomachs...Is there not something dubious and unsatisfactory about a powerful, authoritative system that finds it better to get sick in upper and middle class fashion than in lower class fashion? (p. 10)

It can be seen that the culturalists will minimize the significance of the data indicating a higher rate of schizophrenia in the lower class by maintaining that, first of all, it is the psychiatrist's class-bound values which cause him to label perfectly normal lower class behavior as indicative of mental illness. And, secondly, even if that behavior is an indication of mental illness, it is the psychiatrist's class-bound values that lead him to conclude that lower class forms of mental illness are more of a problem than middle class forms of mental illness, which, in fact, in both cases are class-bound methods of reacting to emotional stress. Whether or not these critics are aware of it (and much as they might deny it), their critiques are, as has been shown, thoroughly grounded in the cultural perspective of poverty, which views the lower class as having its distinct patterns of behavior and values.

It must be pointed out, however, that a cultural perspective does not necessarily lead to the same conclusion to which Szasz, Goffman, and Honigmann arrive. Other culturalists may explain the data differently.

For example, Edward C. Banfield (1970) is a culturalist who asserts a very different and controversial position. To Banfield, not only is there a lower class culture which is different from middle class culture, but that lower class culture is also pathological. He goes so far as to write:

> In the chapters that follow, the term *normal* will be used to refer to class culture that is not lower class. The implication that lower class culture is pathological seems fully warranted both because of the relatively high incidence of mental illness in the lower class and also because human nature seems loath to accept a style of life that is so radically present-oriented. (p. 54)

There are, however, strong grounds for questioning such arguments as Honiggmann's. Roman and Trice (1967), for example, maintain that the argument is irrelevant because the definition of schizophrenia is so diagnosed by a psychiatrist. "The criteria for this definition may include behaviors which are typical outcomes of lower class socialization. This correlation does not decrease the validity of these criteria, since the validity is established by the action of labeling" (p. 44). Furthermore, they contend, this criticism assumes that social classes differ in their conceptions as to what is normal and what is abnormal. Yet several studies across class lines have found no class difference in the determination of behavior as indicative of mental disorder.[5] Finally, in his critical evaluation of the whole approach which explains mental illness as the product of societal reaction, Walter Gove (1970) finds the available evidence indicating "that the vast majority of persons who became patients have a serious disturbance, and it is only when the situation becomes untenable that action is taken" (p. 879). While Gove does not deal directly with the higher incidence of mental illness in the lower class, his findings render those we have labeled culturalists as incorrect as the broader societal reaction approach.

EDUCATION

The literature on the relationship between poverty and education clearly documents the lower class child's confrontation with serious difficulties in the school situation. And this is not a new phenomenon. In her classic study of the subject, Patricia Sexton (1961) spelled out the critical relationship between education and income, by showing that one's education has a great effect on income and on job security (p. 14), that income is directly related to achievement level as measured by the Iowa Achieve-

---

[5] See S. Parker and R. J. Kleiner, "Social Mobility and Mental Illness in an Urban Population," and R. U. Lemkau and G. M. Crocetti, "An Urban Population's Opinion and Knowledge About Mental Illness" (both cited in Roman & Trice, 1967).

ment Test (p. 26), that IQ test scores and income are directly related (p. 39), that the elementary school dropout rate is inversely related to income (p. 97), and that the rate of school attendance and income are directly related (p. 99).

One of the earliest and most influential of the recent explanations of the problems which children of the lower class face in the area of education is that of Allison Davis (1948). Davis maintains that the "social-class patterning of the child's learning, as exerted through the family, extends from the control of the types of food he eats and of the way he eats it to the kinds of sexual, aggressive, and educational training he receives" (p. 12). He refers to an earlier study which he conducted together with Robert J. Havighurst (Havighurst, 1946) and his study with John Dollard (Davis & Dollard, 1964), which found that "as compared with the rearing of middle class children, the early training environment of most lower class children permits them fuller gratification of their organically based drives" (Davis & Dollard, 1964, p. 18). In addition, Davis finds important differences in the "motivational structure" of lower class children as compared to that of middle class, which, in turn, is related to the differences in the adult motivational systems of the two classes. A basic motivational difference is in the attitudes of class members to eating. Because of insecure food supplies, the lower class develops "food anxiety." For similar reasons, they develop anxiety of eviction, of too little sleep, of being cold, and of darkness. Because of these anxieties, when they do get large sums of money, members of the lower class spend it in a manner that seems extravagant to the middle class. They don't adopt the middle class pattern of deferred gratification.

The lower class adult teaches his child to be anxious of social dangers, just as the middle class adult teaches his child; the social dangers, however, differ. "Whereas the middle class child learns a socially adaptive fear of receiving poor grades in school, of being aggressive toward the teacher, of fighting, of cursing, and of having early sex relations, the slum child learns to fear quite different social acts" (Davis, 1948, p. 30). His gang, in fact, teaches him to fear exactly the opposite of what the middle class child fears. "His gang teaches him to fear being taken in by the teacher, of being a softie with her. To study homework seriously is literally a disgrace. Instead of boasting of good marks in school, one conceals them, if he ever receives any." The lower class individual, therefore, cannot be seen as an individual with no anxieties and no social pressures. On the contrary, "society raises many anxieties in slum people also, but with regard to the attainment of what seem to middle class people to be strange goals. *For those who must live in a slum community, however, these goals are realistic and adaptive*" (p. 30, emphasis added).

Lower class "culture" not only influences the emotional systems of its members, it also "guides [their] mental activities" (Davis, 1948, p. 38).

Using an item analysis of 10 intelligence tests, Davis found "that a large proportion of the items in each of these tests "discriminated between" children from the highest and lowest socioeconomic levels" (p. 41).

Davis' explanation of the discrimination is that the tests are not culture-free, but subtly and definitely culture-biased. They are biased because they judge on the basis of language, dialects, and selection of problems that are standard in the middle class. Essentially the same problem exists with respect to the entire school system, maintains Davis. "The school culture itself is a narrow selection of a few highly traditional activities and skills, arbitrarily taken from *middle class culture* as a broader whole" (Davis, 1948, p. 90). For example, because of the emphasis in school upon early reading skills and intelligence scores, the lower class children, not being able to compete on these tests with middle class children, are separated into the "slower" groups. "Segregated from each other, unable therefore either to stimulate or imitate each other, each group fails to learn well those problem-solving activities and insights in which the other group excels. Both groups lose more than they gain" (p. 96).

In terms of his explanation of the source of the problem, therefore, Davis is basically a culturalist, in that he sees a lower class culture which is distinctly different from middle class culture. In terms of his suggestions as to what to do about the problem however, Davis interestingly leans in the direction of the situationalists, in that he recommends altering the situation, the structural framework of the educational system. We shall now look at a number of other studies implicitly based on a cultural approach, in that they trace the problem to aspects of lower class socialization, and then we shall turn to situational explanations.

Arnold W. Green (1946) maintains that the middle class boy is more closely supervised by his mother and, as a result, he undergoes "personality absorption" which makes him more dependent upon adult authority and thus better prepared to cooperate with teachers than lower class boys who are generally less well supervised.

Jackson Toby (1957) traces the better performance of middle class children in school to the expectations of their parents and friends that they do well in school, to their parents' reinforcement of the authority and prestige of the teacher, to their parents' better education and, hence, better ability to help the child with his school work, and to the better skills acquired in middle class child training which prepare him for school work.

Basil Bernstein (1967) concentrates his attention on the differences in language patterns between the lower and middle classes and their relationship to learning. He holds that forms of spoken language in the process of learning initiate, generalize, and reinforce special types of relationships with the environment, and thus create for the individual particular dimensions of significance (p. 179). He divides language into two forms of communication codes, which he labels "the restricted code" and "the elaborated code." The restricted code is for such things as ritualistic modes of communication whereas an elaborated code is universalistic with reference to its meaning inasmuch as it summarizes general social means and ends. A restricted code is particularistic with reference to its meaning inasmuch as it summarizes general social means and ends (pp. 180-181).

The elaborated codes are directed to specific situations and individualized, and their preciseness allows for a complex range of thought, whereas the restricted codes are briefer and less precise, and their meaning is implicit and commonly shared. The restricted codes are most commonly used in impersonal situations.

Bernstein maintains that the codes of communication affect the patterns of relation with others. Language expresses social relations and is then molded by these relations. Language is, thus, an essential aspect in social interaction.

The middle class and lower class, he finds, differ with respect to the way language is used in social control. Control in the lower class, especially in the family, is based on *status* appeal, whereas in the middle class it is *person* oriented. Status appeals are those that "transmit the culture or local culture in such a way as to increase the similarity of the regulated with others of his group" (Bernstein, 1964, p. 200). Noncompliance means rebellion against the culture, and this is what brings on the punishment. And, "the social context of control is such that the relationship is unambiguous—the relative statuses are clear-cut." Person-oriented appeals, by contrast, are oriented to the feelings of the regulator. In this situation, the regulator (for example, the parent) relates the meaning of the act to the child directly, personally. The objective is to justify behavior either in terms of the feelings of the regulator or by having the child identify personally with his action and its consequences. Examples of person-oriented appeals are: "Daddy will be upset if you do that," or "If you break your toy, you'll be sorry because you won't have anything to play with." In the first case the appeal is based upon the feelings—upset—of the father; in the second the appeal is personal in that the child is made to recognize and reckon with the consequences of his act.

The restricted code, because it involves a "rigidity of syntax" and limited "use of structural possibilities for sentence organization, is highly predictable and may be termed a *public* language" (Bernstein, 1962). The person-oriented code, on the other hand, is a *formal* language, because "the structure and syntax are relatively difficult to predict for any one individual and...the formal possibilities of sentence organization are used to clarify meaning and make it explicit" (p. 291).

The values within the middle class, Bernstein maintains, give rise to the carefully ordered universe of the child. Language contributes to this in many ways; for example, authority is related to a stable system of rewards and punishments. The child is an individual in his own right, and his behavior is carefully observed and commented upon. In addition, the child learns to respond to the very personal qualifications used in the language structure. All this helps prepare the middle class child for the school situation, both in terms of his inquisitiveness and eagerness to learn, and in his acceptance of the authority of the teacher.

In the lower class, however, authority appears to the child as arbitrary. The present has greater value than the future goals. The child is limited in his perception of time. Use of the restricted code of communication means that "subjective intent is not verbally explicit or elaborated" (p. 297). Despite the fact that the lower class child might use the very same words as the middle class child, the way he relates the words is different. This results in a low level of conceptualization and limited curiosity.

As a result of these different usages of language and their effects on the intellectual development of the child, the lower class child is, even before he enters school, at a disadvantage in terms of his ability to learn in a situation which requires the attributes of the middle class. Thus, Green, Toby, and Bernstein, as did Davis, trace the source of the problem of the lower class child in school to aspects of lower class socialization and lower class culture. We should caution that Bernstein, however, was writing of differences in lower and middle class language *in England*, not the United States. We have included his work because it has been adopted and become quite influential in America (see Bereiter, 1968; John, 1963; John & Goldstein, 1964). Bereiter (1968) has gone so far as to develop a preschool program based on the assumption that lower class children have no language at all. Vera P. John (1966) has cautioned against the tendency of Bereiter and others to overstress the findings of Bernstein. She emphasizes that Bernstein's work was conducted in England, whereas in the United States "we are witnessing...many thrusts among the poor and the controlled for an extension, instead of a total eclipse of their power" (p. 6). As a result of the differences between the relation of the poor to the power structures in England and in the United States, it is quite possible that the functions of language differ. Thus, she is giving a definite situational or structural interpretation to the findings of Bernstein by maintaining that the differences which Bernstein found in the lower class use of language in England are the result of the position which the lower class occupies and the degree to which it is "eclipsed" from "the power structure" in England. These findings, she says, do not necessarily relate to the United States, where, she maintains, there are significant changes taking place insofar as the "relation of the poor to the power structure." In addition, she argues, in the United States there is "an increasing poverty of language as a means of communication" among the non-poor as the result of "pre-packaged messages, untapped by multiple-choice exams, and impoverished by the repetitious impact of the mass media" (p. 10).

Whereas Bernstein makes no such distinctions between England and the United States, he has recently been critical of the concepts "compensatory education" and "cultural deprivation," which have been derived from his earlier work. His criticism of these concepts does not, however, remove him from the culturalist school. Rather, though he remains a culturalist, he recognizes that focusing upon the families and the children "distracts attention from the deficiencies in the school itself" (1974, p. 111). Moreover, while middle-class children are socialized to universalistic meanings and lower class children to particularistic meanings, "this does not mean that working-class mothers are non-verbal." Rather, "they differ from middle class mothers in the *contexts* which evoke universalistic meanings. They are *not* linguistically deprived, neither are their children" (p. 117). Bernstein argues that instead of deliberately trying to change the child's dialect, the teacher should first try to understand it. "If the culture of the teacher is to become part of the consciousness of the child, then the culture of the child must be in the consciousness of the teacher" (p. 120). Thus, similar to Allison Davis, Bernstein is a culturalist in his explanation and a structuralist in terms of dealing with it.

The questions as to whether Bernstein's explanation is applicable to the United States and whether John's explanation of Bernstein's findings is adequate shall be left open. The essential point for our purposes is that Bernstein's approach follows that of Davis, Green, Toby, and others who find the source of the problems of lower class children in school to lie in aspects of lower class culture. For this reason, we have grouped them as culturalists. The basic assumptions of this approach have been clearly formulated by Martin P. Deutch (1964).

> We know that children from underprivileged environments tend to come to school with qualitatively different preparation for the demands of both the learning process and the behavioral equipments of the classroom. There are various differences in the kinds of socializing experiences these children have had, as contrasted with the middle class child. The culture of their environment is a different one from the culture that has molded the school and its educational techniques and theories. (p. 172)

FAMILY LIFE

There is a clear relationship between social class and the number of children in the family. Specifically, the lower class has the highest birthrate and the greatest number of children in the family. Lee Rainwater (1960), for example, in his study of "Sex, Contraception, and Family Planning in the Working Class," found that "the lower the status...the more children the respondents have, and the more they expect" (p. 25).

When the patterns of the parent-child relationship in different social classes are examined, it is found that there are significant differences in the socialization patterns of the lower class as compared to the middle class. First of all, we find that the foci of the families are different. In the lower class, the families are adult-centered and the parent-child relationship is very segregated. Herbert Gans, in his study of the white working class in the West End of Boston (1962), described the relationship as follows:

> The child will report on his peer-group activities at home, but they are of relatively little interest to parents in an adult-centered family. If the child performs well at school, parents will praise him for it, but they are unlikely to attend his performance in a school program or a baseball game in person. This is his life, not theirs.[6]

This contrasts sharply with the child-centered relationship which characterizes the middle class (see Seeley, Sim, & Loosely, 1963).

Moreover, the differences extend to child-rearing practices. Thus we find that, for example, in a well-known study, Urie Bronfenbrenner (1958) investigated the changes in patterns of socialization in the 25 years between 1930 and 1955, and found an increasing permissiveness in the feeding and toilet-training practices of middle class mothers. Despite these changes in practices, however, these middle class mothers have not correspondingly altered their expectations as to their children's performance. Rather, they have changed in the methods which they use to have their children live up to their expectations. "They reason with the youngster, isolate him, appeal to guilt, show disappointment—in short, convey in a variety of ways, on the one hand, the kind of behavior that is expected of the child; on the other, the realization that transgression means the interruption of a mutually valued relationship" (p. 49).

Bronfenbrenner found the most important source of the changes to be in the access to agents of social change. "Taken together, the findings on changes in infant care lead to the generalization that socialization practices are most likely to be altered in those segments of society which have most ready access to the agencies or agents of social change (e.g., books, pamphlets, physicians, and counselors" (p. 424).

---

[6] It should be noted that Gans' description is of the working class, not, strictly speaking, the lower class. However, the assumption that this pattern is also, if not more so, characteristic of the lower class, is implicit in Gans and explicit in the works of many who compare this pattern to the pattern typical in the middle class. In a study of children of lower class families (Pavenstedt, 1967), Louise S. Bandler describes the parent-child relationship ("Family Functioning: A Psychosocial Perspective," pp. 225-253), and reports that "[t]he mother's involvement in such activities as play with the children was absent." Also, among the major traits of the culture of poverty on the family level, Oscar Lewis (1966) lists "the absence of childhood as a specially prolonged and protected stage in the lifecycle" (p. xlvii).

Table 1.3 *Overall character of parent-child relationship*

Sample	Approx. date of practice	No. of cases reported	Age	Middle-class trend	Working-class trend
Berkeley I	1928-32	31	1-3	Grants autonomy Cooperative Equalitarian	Expresses affection Excessive contact Intrusive Irritable Punitive Ignores child
National I	1932	494	0-1		Baby picked up when cries†
National IV	1932	3239	1-12	Higher percentage of children punished†	Nothing done to allay child's fears†
Yellow Springs, Ohio	1940	124	3-12	Acceptant-democratic	Indulgent
Berkeley II	1939-42	31	9-11	Grants autonomy Cooperative Equalitarian Expresses affection	Active-rejectant Excessive contact Intrusive Irritable Punitive Ignores child
Chicago I	1943	100	5		Father plays with child more†
Chicago II	1943-44	433	1-5	"Developmental" conception of "good mother" and "good child."†	"Traditional" conception of "good mother" and "good child."†
New Haven I	1949-50	219	1	More necessary discipline to prevent injury or danger.†	More prohibitive discipline beyond risk of danger or injury.
Boston	1951-52	372	5	Mother warmer toward child† Father warmer toward child* Father exercises more authority* Mother has higher esteem for father† Mother delighted about pregnancy† Both parents more often share authority*	Father demands instant obedience† Child ridiculed† Greater rejection of child† Emphasis on neatness, cleanliness, and order† Parents disagree more on child-rearing policy*
New Haven II	1951-53	48	14-17	Fathers have more power in family decisions† Parents agree in value orientations†	
Palo Alto	1953	73	2½—5½	Baby picked up when cries†	Mother carries through demands rather than dropping the subject†
Eugene	1955-56	206	0-18	Better relationship between father and child†	
Washington, D.C.	1956-57	400	10-11	Desirable qualities are happiness,* considerateness,* curiosity,* self-control*	Desirable qualities are neatness-cleanliness,* obedience*

*Trend significant at 5-percent level or better.
†The difference between percentages is not significant but the difference between mean ratings is significant at the 5-percent level or better.
Source: Urie Bronfenbrenner, "Socialization and Social Class Through Time and Space." From READINGS IN SOCIAL PSYCHOLOGY, Third Edition, Edited by Eleanor E. Maccoby, Theodore M. Newcomb, and Eugene L. Hartley, Copyright 1947, 1952 © 1958 by Holt, Rinehart & Winston, Inc. Reprinted by permission of Holt, Rinehart & Winston.

Table 1.3 indicates differences in the "Overall Character of Parent-Child Relationship" as found by Bronfenbrenner in the middle and lower classes.

Melvin L. Kohn (1959), noting the studies of Bronfenbrenner and those to which he referred, attempted to interpret the relationship between social class and the exercise of parental authority. He stratified his sample of 400 families in accordance with the Hollingshead Index of Social Position and questioned them as to paternal and maternal authority and the use of physical punishment. He found that the parents of neither class resort to punishment initially, but they do so only after their children fail to heed their warnings. The difference between the punishment of middle class parents and working class parents lies in that to which the parents in each class react. "Working class parents are more likely to respond in terms of the immediate consequences of the child's actions, middle class parents in terms of their interpretation of the child's intent in acting as he does" (p. 364). This difference Kohn relates to the priority of values of parents in both of the classes. We shall look at the question of differences in values below.

Further evidence of the relationship between poverty, education, and several characteristics of family composition may be seen in Tables 1.4 and 1.5.

As these tables and the other data presented clearly indicate, there are a number of aspects of family life in the lower class which are significantly different from those in the middle class. The lower class has a higher birthrate, larger families, different overall pattern of parent-child relationship, and particularly different patterns of socialization than does the middle class. Over the facts themselves there is little disagreement. The explanation, however, is another matter.

On the matter of the higher birthrate in the lower class, Lee Rainwater (1960) concludes that "the lack of effective contraception so common in this group is not due simply to ignorance and misunderstanding; *it is embodied in particular personalities, world views, and ways of life which have consistency and stability and which do not readily admit such foreign elements as conscious planning and emotion-laden contraceptive practices*" (pp. 167-188, emphasis in original).

Contrary to the popular stereotype of the lower class, these world views and ways of life do not involve the lack of social controls in the area of sex, "hypersex," and promiscuity, but rather very rigid attitudes involving shame and embarrassment, "reminiscent of a Victorian attitude" (H. Lewis, 1967a, p. 9; also see Handel & Rainwater, 1961; Rainwater, 1960). Gerald Handel and Lee Rainwater (1961) found, in addition, that one of the reasons for lack of contraception arises over many lower class

Table 1.4 *Selected characteristics of all families and of poor families, 1962*

Selected characteristic	Number of families (millions)		Percent of total	
	All families	Poor families	All families	Poor families
Total	47.0	9.3	100	100
Age of head:				
14-24 years	2.5	.8	5	8
25-54 years	30.4	3.9	65	42
55-64 years	7.3	1.4	16	15
65 years and over	6.8	3.2	14	34
Education of head:[1]				
8 years or less	16.3	6.0	35	61
9-11 years	8.6	1.7	19	17
12 years	12.2	1.5	26	15
More than 12 years	9.3	.7	20	7
Sex of head:				
Male	42.3	7.0	90	75
Female	4.7	2.3	10	25
Labor force status of head:[2]				
Not in civilian labor force	8.4	4.1	18	44
Employed	36.9	4.6	78	49
Unemployed	1.7	.6	4	6
Color of family:				
White	42.4	7.3	90	78
Nonwhite	4.6	2.0	10	22
Children under 18 years of age in family:				
None	18.8	4.9	40	52
One to three	22.7	3.3	48	36
Four or more	5.5	1.1	12	11
Earners in family:				
None	3.8	2.8	8	30
One	21.1	4.3	45	46
Two or more	22.1	2.2	47	23
Regional location of family:[3,4]				
Northeast	11.5	1.6	25	17
North Central	13.1	2.3	29	25
South	13.5	4.3	30	47
West	7.0	1.0	16	11
Residence of family:[4,5]				
Rural farm	3.3	1.5	7	16
Rural nonfarm	9.9	2.7	22	30
Urban	31.9	5.0	71	54

[1]Based on 1961 income (1962 prices).
[2]Labor force status relates to survey week of March 1963.
[3]Based on 1960 residence and 1959 income (1962 prices).
[4]Data are from 1960 Census and are therefore not strictly comparable with the other data shown in this table, which are derived from *Current Population Reports*.
[5]Based on 1959 residence and 1959 income (1962 prices).

NOTE.—Data relate to families and exclude unrelated individuals. Poor families are defined as all families with total money income of less than $3,000.

Source: Department of Commerce and Council of Economic Advisers. *Economic Report to the President.* Washington, D.C.; United States Government Printing Office, 1964, p. 61.

Table 1.5 *Number of families and incidence of poverty, by education and other selected characteristics, 1959*

Selected characteristic	Number of families (thousands)	Incidence of poverty (percent)				
		Total	Years of school completed			
			8 years or less	9 to 11 years	12 years	More than 12 years
All families[1]	45,150	21	35	18	12	8
White families	40,887	19	31	15	11	7
Head under 25 years of age	2,114	28	45	33	22	22
Husband-wife families	1,964	25	42	28	20	20
Female head	112	77	85	86	68	60
Head 25 to 64 years of age	33,164	13	23	12	8	6
Husband-wife families	30,067	11	21	9	6	4
Female head	2,344	42	51	46	36	23
Head 65 years old or older	5,609	46	53	39	33	24
Husband-wife families	4,434	48	55	39	34	23
Female head	849	42	46	40	33	28
Nonwhite families	4,263	48	57	42	30	18
Head under 25 years of age	242	64	76	66	51	40
Husband-wife families	178	57	71	56	45	42
Female head	55	89	94	92	83	50
Head 25 to 64 years of age	3,527	43	53	38	27	15
Husband-wife families	2,680	36	47	26	18	11
Female head	713	72	77	73	62	39
Head 65 years old or older	494	71	74	52	50	41
Husband-wife families	335	70	73	53	45	42
Female head	123	76	79	63	75	50

[1]Include "husband-wife" families, "female head" families, and "other male head" families. Husband-wife families are those in which both spouses are present. Female head families are those with no male spouse present. Other male head families are those with no female spouse present; this family type is excluded from the detail of table but is included in the totals for color and age.

NOTE.—Data relate to families and exclude unrelated individuals. Poor families are defined as all families with total money income of less than $3.000 in 1959. Since the data in this table relate to income in 1959 prices, they are not strictly comparable with data in other poverty tables in this Report, which are based on income in 1962 prices. Incidence of poverty is measured by the percent that poor families with a given combination of characteristics are of all families with the same combination of characteristics.

Source: Department of Commerce and Council of Economic Advisers. *Economic Report to the President.* Washington, D.C.; United States government Printing Office, 1964, p. 83.

couples' disagreement over which partner is responsible for contraception. They are "unable to get beyond the polarized position of each insisting that the other should take the responsibility" (p. 24). A third reason, they found, lies in the passive role which many lower class women play in sexual relations, precluding their consideration of any method of birth control which might interfere with their male partner's pleasure.

Up to this point, four characteristics of the poor have been established, and it has been shown that with each of these there are theorists who explain these characteristics in terms of the cultural perspective. Before concluding this chapter, however, the discussion must be rounded out with some attention given to the social policy suggestions which have derived from this cultural perspective.

The details shall be elaborated upon in a later chapter; at this juncture, suffice it to say that almost the entire field of social work until recently, and especially the social casework approach, was predicated upon a cultural perspective in which the problems of the poor are seen as deriving from internal sources. The notion of "helping the poor to help themselves" implies, basically, that the poor have to be changed to fit the system, which is, again implicitly, sound. In this line of reasoning, the poor can only hope to improve their lot by adopting the values and patterns of behavior of the non-poor. Helping the poor means helping them to think and behave "properly." In order to accomplish this monumental task of changing the poor, drastic measures may be required. Thus, for example, the Job Corps, one of the components of the Economic Opportunity Act of 1964, the "War on Poverty," which was addressed to the area of employment, was designed to offer a basic education and marketable skills to its enrollees. It was, however, based upon a rigid version of the cultural perspective, for it assumed that the youth had to be removed from his ("vicious") environment if the training program was to be effective.

To cite one more example, the major component of the Economic Opportunity Act of 1964 dealing with education was the much-publicized Project Head Start. The basic assumptions of the cultural perspective as they relate to the area of education and the poor have been summed up by Martin Deutch, as was cited above in the concluding paragraph of the section discussing "Education," and it is on the basis of these assumptions that Project Head Start was initiated. As J. McVicker Hunt (1969) puts it:

> Various lines of evidence show that it becomes increasingly difficult to alter the effects of early experience the longer the young organism has encountered a given kind of circumstance. It follows that corrective efforts should be focused upon the young, and preferably upon the very young. The evidence we have suggests

> that early childhood education can have tremendous social significance if we learn how to do it effectively...Project Head Start is a tremendous step in the right direction. (p. 137)

In sum, the culturalists see the poor as manifesting unique patterns of behavior and values; to escape from their poverty, they must be taught to change their behavior and values. Since their values and patterns of behavior have been internalized over generations through socialization, the change will, of necessity, be a slow and difficult process.

Chapter 2

THE SITUATIONAL PERSPECTIVE

In contrast to the cultural perspective, there is the alternative situational or structural perspective according to which the poor are viewed in a very different light. Granting that the poor do manifest statistically unique patterns of behavior, the situationalist argues that these derive not internally, generated by the unique values of the poor, but rather, externally, as the inevitable consequence of their occupying an unfavorable position in a restrictive social structure. The poor behave differently not because they possess their own unique value system, but, on the contrary, because they have internalized the dominant values but do not have the opportunity to realize these values through the socially sanctioned avenues. To effect a change insofar as poverty is concerned, the situationalists argue, requires not changing the poor themselves, but rather changing their situation by correcting the restrictive social structure.

As was the procedure in the previous chapter, this chapter will demonstrate and examine the situational perspective as it pertains to the four selected variables and will conclude with the implications of this perspective for social policy. Also, as in the previous chapter, our analysis is not concerned with the causal relationship between this, the situational model, and each of the variables. Rather, we are concerned with the ideological view of the poor implicit in the situational model which supports the stigmatization of the poor and carries with it certain social policy assumptions.

CRIME

One of the most influential explanations of the relationship between poverty and crime is that of Robert K. Merton (1938), in his article "Social Structure and Anomie." In an attempt to discover "how some social structures exert a definite pressure upon certain persons in the society to engage in nonconformist rather that conformist conduct" (p. 671), Merton singles out for analysis two elements of the social and cultural structure—cultural goals and institutional norms. Social and cultural integration can occur only when there is relative equilibrium between these two components of the structure. When there is disproportionate stress on one or the other, social and cultural malintegration results. Specifically, when "certain aspects of the social structure...generate countermores and antisocial behavior precisely because of the differential emphases on goals and regulations," then "the integration of the society becomes tenuous and anomie ensues" (p. 674).

In regard to the correlation between poverty and crime, Merton maintains that poverty and lack of opportunities in and of themselves do not cause crime. "Poverty," he argues, "is not an isolated variable" (p. 680), and "poverty as such, and consequent limitation of opportunity, are not sufficient to induce a conspicuously high rate of criminal behavior" (p. 681). In fact, there are areas in southeastern Europe which have high poverty rates with very limited opportunities for vertical mobility that do not have correspondingly high crime rates. So there must be something about poverty and its meaning in the United States which is the source of the high crime rates among the poor. The answer, Merton maintains, lies in certain unique aspects of American culture.

A major aspect of American culture, says Merton, is the high premium it places on economic affluence for all. Americans are admonished to succeed, and success is defined and demonstrated in terms of pecuniary success. This success ideology prevails through the social structure; it is internalized by all the strata. "These goals are held to *transcend class lines*" (p. 680). At the same time that the goal is internalized by all the strata, however, "the actual social organization is such that there exist class differentials in the accessibility of these *common* success-symbols" (p. 680). The farther down one goes in the stratification system, the more one is confronted with restrictions in terms of the availability of legitimate means for achieving the success goal. This conflict between culture goals—success, and the institutionalized means available for achieving them, leads to anomie. "Frustration and thwarted aspiration lead to the search for avenues of escape from a culturally induced intolerable situation; or unrelieved ambition may eventuate in illicit attempts to acquire the dominant values" (p. 680). Thus, as the evidence from sections of southeastern Europe indicates, poverty and deprivation in and of themselves do not necessarily lead to crime. The high correlation between poverty and crime in the United States is due to the unique aspect of American culture which gives poverty a special meaning, and this induces criminal behavior. "It is only when the full configuration is considered, poverty, limited opportunity and a commonly shared system of success symbols, that we can explain the higher association between poverty and crime in our society than in others where rigidified class structure is coupled with differential class symbols of achievement" (p. 681).

This theory, perhaps more than any other, has guided the course of theory and policy concerning crime and poverty in American society. And yet, it is open to much criticism. Bernard and Nathan Lander (1964) take issue with Merton's basic postulate concerning the all-pervasiveness of the success goal, and maintain that the evidence, for example from Ely Chinoy's study of *Automobile Workers and the American Dream* (1955) indicates that factory workers do not, in fact, aspire to the higher echelons of business and industry. Furthermore, Merton's theory does not account for the recent dramatic rises in rural delinquency, suburban delinquency, and middle class delinquency. And, Merton does not account for the wide variations in delinquency rates among working class neighborhoods.

In a recent study by Bernard Rosenberg and Harry Silverstein (1969), designed to test some of the questions raised by the Landers, the authors found that in all three of the areas they studied (New York City, Washington, D.C., and Chicago) the lower class youth did not aspire to any unrealistic goals. "On the contrary...social and economic realism is the rule. High aspiration among the three impoverished groups of youth in our study is almost nonexistent" (p. 125). With all of the criticisms, however, Merton's remains a major structural explanation.

Much of the research in American criminology has focused upon juvenile delinquency—particulary, gang delinquency—and one of the most prominent approaches to this problem has been the cultural transmission perspective. Despite its name, it will be shown that the cultural transmission perspective is clearly part of the broader situational perspective. It is a product of the Chicago school and has its roots in the pioneering study of Frederick M. Thrasher, *The Gang*, published in 1927.[7] Thrasher summed up his hypothesis in the last paragraph of his introduction:

> Gangs like most other social groups, originate under conditions that are typical for all groups of the same species; they develop in definite and predictable ways, in accordance with a form or entelechy that is predetermined by characteristic internal processes and mechanisms, and have, in short, a nature and a natural history.

On the basis of his investigation of 1,313 gangs in Chicago, Thrasher found that "gangland represents a geographically and socially interstitial area in the city" (p. 20), that is, that gangs are characteristic of a slum area, Zone II, the "zone in transition" in the Park and Burgess concentric zone hypothesis. The interstitial area is characterized by "deteriorating neighborhoods, shifting populations, and the mobility and disorganization of

[7] All references are to the abridged edition, University of Chicago Press, 1963.

the slum" (p. 20). In this interstitial area, "gangs in embryo," or spontaneous play groups are constantly forming, and the density of the area presents a full range of opportunities for conflict with antagonists within and outside of the gang. There is conflict between gangs over the domain, rights, and privileges of each, and there is conflict between the gang and the "conventional social order" over the latter's opposition to the gang's independence, its non-control by the conventional social order. From this latter form of conflict there arises an antagonism between some of the gangs and all symbols of authority in the conventional social order—police, parents, teachers, merchants, etc. Those gangs that persist continue their efforts to cast off the conventional restraints, become aligned with similar gangs, become increasingly involved in intergroup fighting and illegal activities, and increasingly attempt to derive "the thrill and zest of participation in common interests, more especially in corporate action, in hunting, capture, conflict, flight, and escape" (p. 32).

The roots of the gang lie "in the spontaneous effort of boys and girls to create a society for themselves where none adequate to their needs exists" (p. 32). We can immediately see that what Thrasher is saying is that the gang, while it is part of a subculture, remains always a situational adaptation, in that it is a reaction to a dominant structure which is inadequate to the slum boys' needs. Thrasher later elaborates on this important point:

> *The gang develops as a response to society.* The social group of which the gang boy is a member has failed to provide organized and supervised activities adequate to absorb his interests and exhaust his energies. An active boy without an outlet for his energies is a restless boy—seeking satisfactions he cannot name, willing to experiment, curious about this and that, eager to escape whatever surveillance is placed upon him. *The gang solves his problem offering him what society has failed to provide.* (p. 117, emphasis added)

The gang offers the boy organization—it acts as a unit, develops social patterns and codes, inner social control, discipline, division of labor, opportunities for leadership—in short, social structure and social patterns (p. 179ff).

Thrasher then makes the intriguing observation that while the gang is, as we stated, a subculture which is a situational adaptation to an inadequate dominant social structure, it is also a microcosm of the larger neighborhood, which is a subculture apart from the non-slum culture. He states that "the gang is not divorced from larger social controls. Without formal and conventional control, yet *it reflects in its activities the adult life and the customs of the particular community where it is found*" (p. 178, emphasis added). Thus, the gang is simultaneously a reflection, a subculture within the subculture of "the particular community where it is found," which is, in turn, a subdivision of the larger societal culture, and, at the same time, the gang forms as a reaction to the inadequate larger society.

Following in the tradition of Thrasher, Albert K. Cohen introduced the concept of subculture in the sociological analysis of juvenile delinquency in 1955, with the publication of his book, *Delinquent Boys*, subtitled *The Culture of the Gang*. Cohen defined subculture as a subdivision of large-scale national cultures: "Every society is internally differentiated into numerous sub-groups, each with its ways of thinking and doing that are in some respects peculiarly its own, that one can acquire only one by participating in these sub-groups and that one can scarcely help acquiring if he is a full-fledged participant. These cultures within cultures are 'subcultures' " (1955, p. 12). A delinquent subculture, to Cohen, refers to

> a way of life that has somehow become traditional among certain groups in American society. These groups are the boys' gangs that flourish most conspicuously in the "delinquent neighborhoods" of our larger American cities. The members of these gangs grow up, some to become law-abiding citizens and others to graduate to more professional and adult forms of criminality, but the delinquent tradition is kept alive by the age-groups that succeed them. (p. 13)

Cohen distinguishes between gang delinquency and adult criminality in that whereas the latter is primarily directed to a utilitarian goal—profit—gang delinquency is primarily "non-utilitarian, malicious and negativistic" (p. 25). Moreover, whereas adult criminality is usually carefully planned and the adult criminal usually specializes in a particular type of crime, gang delinquency is characteristically diversified and the delinquent is typically one who has no patience for planning and doesn't seem to care about the consequences (pp. 25-30).

Cohen then makes an observation that seems to echo that of Thrasher; he states that "short-lived hedonism is not characteristic of delinquent gangs alone. On the contrary, it is common throughout the social class from which delinquents characteristically come. However, in the delinquent gang it reaches its finest flower. It is the fabric, as it were, of which delinquency is the most brilliant and spectacular thread" (pp. 30-31). As did Thrasher, Cohen appears to be saying that the delinquent subculture is a reflection of the general lower class subculture of which it is a part. We say that this is what he "appears to be saying" because he states this only as a passing remark, and the analysis which follows takes a very different track.

Cohen's explanation of the delinquent subculture is that it is one of three responses to situations of stress which arise from the lower class boy's having to compete for status in terms of middle class standards. Specifically, he maintains that lower class children are socialized to live up to lower class standards and develop a lower class personality.[8]

The problem arises for the lower class child, however, when he is confronted with a situation in which he must compete with middle class children for status in terms of middle class criteria (for example, in school). In such situations the lower class boy is invariably at the bottom of the status heap; he is a failure.

To resolve this dilemma, the lower class boy may choose one of three alternatives. He may adopt the "college boy" response—that is, he may reject his lower class way of life and, with great sacrifice, strive to meet the middle class standards (this response would seem to be the one which is now pejoratively called the "Uncle Tom" approach). Or, he may adopt the "stable corner-boy response," whereby the child accepts and tries to make the best of his corner-boy situation. The third response, the delinquent subculture response, is characterized by its "explicit and wholesale repudiation of middle class standards and the adoption of their antithesis" (Cohen, 1955, p. 129). It is not simply a nonconformity to middle class standards; it is the complete rejection and reversal of them. "In terms of the norms of the delinquent subculture, defined by its negative polarity to the respectable status system, the delinquent's very non-conformity to middle class standards set him above the most exemplary college boy" (p. 131). Thus, the very same values which motivate the middle class child to conformity serve as the source of gang delinquency, which is the negative response of the lower class child to middle class standards (pp. 131-137). And, we emphasize, the delinquent subculture, accordingly, persists as one of three continuous reactions or *adaptations to a persisting situation wherein the lower class boy is at a structural disadvantage.*

Two years after the publication of *Delinquent Boys*, Cohen, together with James F. Short, Jr., published an essay (Cohen & Short, 1958) in which they attempted to break down the delinquent subculture into various subcategories; he and Short discussed five types:

The parent male subculture. This refers to the delinquent subculture described in *Delinquent Boys*, as above. It is the parent subculture "because it is probably the most common variety...and because the charac-

---

[8] He "appears to be more dependent upon and at home" in primary groups...He appears to be more spontaneous, emotionally irrepressible and anarchic, to give freer and less disguised expression to his aggression, and to find it more difficult to play roles with which he does not basically identify. He is less likely to possess, to value or to cultivate the polish, the sophistication, the fluency, the 'good appearance' and the 'personality' so useful in 'selling oneself' and manipulating others in the middle class world" (Cohen, 1955, p. 97).

teristics listed above seem to constitute a common core shared by other important variants" (p. 24).

The conflict-oriented subculture. This is the most popular subculture in the sense of its being the most prominent in the news media in the United States today. It is composed of groups of large gangs, numbering as many as several hundred members, which are highly organized in terms of role allocation. The large gang may be divided into subgangs on the basis of age or territory, and there may be alliances with other gangs. They "have a strong sense of corporate identity, a public personality or 'rep' in the gang world" (p. 25). The status of the gang is achieved on the basis of its members' toughness and prowess in "rumbles" with other gangs. Status within the gang is determined primarily by the demonstration of "heart" or courage in fighting, although fighting itself occupies only a small part of the gang's time. There is ambivalence about fighting in that the members do fear the rumbles and may even be relieved when police intervene to prevent it, but, at the same time, the gang demands a suppression of fear and a constant readiness to engage in violence and even brutality in order to defend rep. In its other aspects, this type of gang is similar to that of the delinquent subculture. It engages in drinking, sex, gambling, stealing, vandalism, etc. It is, as is the delinquent subculture, "concentrated in sections of the city that are highly mobile, working-class, impoverished, and characterized by a wide variety of indices of disorganization" (p. 25).

The drug addict subculture. This subculture is distinguished from the first two in that its delinquency is definitely utilitarian; it engages predominantly in profit-making crimes in order to be able to purchase narcotic drugs. It is a subculture in that it "centers around the use of narcotic drugs" which "provides a markedly distinct way of life" (p. 26). Most commonly, the addicts, prior to their addiction, were active members of delinquent gangs, but once they become addicted, they recede to the periphery of these gangs. The addict is of less value to the delinquent gang and therefore has a lower status within them. In time, when the addict subculture achieves autonomy, it has a relatively high status in its community. The addict then moves from the conflict subculture into the world which Harold Finestone (1957) has described as "Cats, Kicks and Color." In the cat subculture, the major theses are the "kick," which Finestone defines as "any act tabooed by 'squares' that heightens and intensifies the present moment of experience and differentiates it as much as possible from the humdrum routine of daily life (quoted by Cohen & Short, 1958, p. 26) and the "hustle," "any non-violent means of making some bread (money) which does not require work" (quoted by Cohen & Short, 1958, p. 26). The cat may be engaged in pimping, petty theft, pickpocketing; he may be a pool shark, or be part of any other "con" activities, but heroin is the ultimate kick, because the pleasure derived from the kick and the hustle lies in the fact that they are tabooed by conventional norms. Heroin is the substance most "profoundly tabooed by conventional middle class society," and "no other 'kick' offers such an instantaneous intensification of the immediate moment of experience and sets it apart from everyday experience in such spectacular fashion" (Finestone, 1957, pp. 5-6). The lifestyle of the cat is described by Finestone as seeking "through a harmonious combination of charm, ingratiating speech, dress, music, the proper dedication to his 'kick,' and unrestrained generosity to make of his day-to-day life itself a gracious work of art. Everything is to be pleasant and everything he does and values is to contribute to a cultivated aesthetic approach to living. The 'cool cat' exemplifies all of these elements in proper balance" (pp. 5-6). The addict subculture is in the most deprived neighborhoods, is typically composed of a group of individuals beyond the age of 16 from "the most-discriminated-against minority groups, especially Negroes" (Cohen & Short, 1958, p. 27).

The semi-professional subculture. This subculture is composed of those boys, age 16 or 17, who have not dropped out of the delinquent subculture, as the majority does, but rather have progressed to more systematic and utilitarian crimes. Patterns in the semi-professional subculture include: "The use of strong arm methods (robbery) of obtaining money; the *sale* of stolen articles, *versus* using for oneself, giving or throwing away, or returning stolen articles; stating, as a reason for continued stealing, 'want things' or 'need money' *versus* stealing for excitement, because others do it, because they like to, or for spite" (Cohen & Short, 1958, p. 27). Cohen and Short speculate that the semi-professional thieves form cliques within larger gangs, are probably differentiated by other characteristics than just patterns of stealing, and "tend to segregate themselves into more professionally oriented and 'serious-minded' groups." (p. 28).

The middle class delinquent subculture. Whereas the delinquent subcultures described above are primarily concentrated in the working class, Cohen and Short theorize, with "no firm basis in research," that middle class delinquency also takes a subcultural form, with subtle but important differences between them and the various working class subcultures. "It seems probable that the qualities of malice, bellicosity, and violence will be underplayed in the middle class subcultures, and that these subcultures will emphasize more the deliberate courting of danger (suggested by the epithet 'chicken') and a more sophisticated, irresponsible, 'playboy' approach to activities symbolic, in our culture, of adult roles and centering largely around sex, liquor, and automobiles" (p. 28).

Several years later Richard A. Cloward and Lloyd E. Ohlin (1960) published their study, *Delinquency and Opportunity*, wherein they maintain that "the delinquent subculture is a special category of deviant subculture...A delinquent subculture is one in which certain forms of delinquent activity are essential requirements for the performance of the dominant roles supported by the subculture" (p. 7). As did Cohen, they see the delinquent subculture as providing an alternate set of norms which replace the conventional norms. "The delinquent subculture called for the withdrawal of sentiments supporting official norms and the tendering of allegiance to competing norms" (p. 20). There are, accordingly, three basic types of delinquent subcultures found among adolescent males in lower class urban American areas.

The criminal subculture. This subculture is based upon criminal values and is the training ground for adult criminality. It is the most extensively described in the sociological literature on delinquency, and involves "a tradition which integrates youthful delinquency and adult criminality" (p. 22). Emphasis is on utilitarian crimes, and success is defined in terms of being able to pull off the "big score." Learning involves not only skills and knowledge essential in the performance of crime, but also respect for adult criminals, adopting the "right guy" as the role model, and acquiring "connections" in the criminal world. The "right guys" and "connections," through their demonstrations of graft and corruption in the so-called law-abiding society, create an attitude for the youngster of "successful people in the conventional world as having a 'racket,'...[and] this attitude successfully neutralizes the controlling effect of the conventional norms" (p. 23).

Cloward and Ohlin continue to analyze two other types of delinquent subcultures—*the conflict subculture*, which is essentially the same as that analyzed by Cohen and Short, and *the retreatist subculture*, which is essentially the same as Cohen and Short's drug-addict subculture, and is also based upon Finestone's description of the "cat" world.

Basically, as was stated previously, all of the theories of delinquent subculture are situational explanations—that is, they explain the lower class delinquency as deriving from the delinquents' reactions to the dominant middle class social and cultural structure. For Thrasher, the gang arises as a response to that which the structure does not provide. To Cohen, gang delinquency is a reaction to and a reversal of middle class standards. And the thesis of Cloward and Ohlin is that delinquent subcultures arise out of the lower class youth's awareness of his very limited access or opportunity to achieve the conventional goals of success through legitimate means; he thus substitutes illegitimate or delinquent means in order to achieve the desired and culturally prescribed goals. The situationalist posits lower class delinquent behavior as a reaction to middle class culture, whereas Walter B. Miller, the culturalist, argues that "it is a by-product of action primarily oriented to the lower class system. The standards of lower class culture cannot be seen as a reverse function of middle class culture..." (W. B. Miller, 1958, p. 19).

In order to avoid the problems involved with the use of official statistics, Albert J. Reiss, Jr. and Albert L. Rhodes (1961) sampled 158 of 9,238 boys age 12 years and over enrolled in junior and senior high school and interviewed them and their friends on such matters as vocational aspirations, behavior (conforming and deviating) of their friends, amount and type of delinquent behavior, and adult supervision of leisure time activities. They found, in fact, a higher rate of delinquency in the lower class. However, and this is in criticism of the delinquent subculture approach, they found that

> there is no simple relationship between ascribed social status and delinquency. Both the status structure of an area and the extent to which delnquency occurs as a cultural tradition affect the delinquency life chance of a boy at each ascribed status level. While the life-chances of low ascribed status boys becoming delinquent are greater than those of high status ones, a low status boy in a predominantly high status area with a low rate of delinquency has almost no chance of being classified a juvenile court delinquent. (p. 729)

Thus the findings of Reiss and Rhodes raise serious doubts as to the contention of delinquent subculture theory, and especially Cohen's, that the high delinquency rates of lower class boys are the result of the pressures of middle class norms, for these should be greatest in a high status area. Rather, the findings of Reiss and Rhodes give general "support to Miller's thesis that delinquency is normative in lower class culture while conformity is normative in middle class culture" (Reiss & Rhodes, 1961, p. 729).

John P. Clark and Eugene P. Wenninger (1962), in a study of 1,154 public school children from sixth through 12th grades in four types of communities, also found the status area factor to be of prime importance. They found that "the lower class areas have higher illegal behavior rates, particularly in the more serious types of offenses," and the important variable is area and the predominant class of that area rather than the class of the delinquent. "The pattern of illegal behavior within small communities or within 'status areas' of a large metropolitan center is determined by the predominant class of that area" (p. 833). Again, this seems to refute Cohen in that the pressure for delinquency should be greatest among lower class youth in a predominantly middle class area, because the incidence of being ranked in terms of middle class standards would be greater than in a predominantly lower class area. Cohen might, however, reply that in a predominantly middle class area there are greater pressures on lower class youth to adopt the "college-boy" pattern. As for Merton, the problem is that in a predominantly middle class area there should be even greater pressures on lower class individuals because the goals to which Merton maintains that he aspires are much more readily apparent than in a predominantly lower class area.

In response to Albert Cohen, David Matza (1964) is critical of the delinquent subculture approach on the grounds that it is a positivistic or a deterministic approach, and fails to "account for the delinquent's frequent conformity to the standards and expectations he allegedly repudiates" (p. 27). Instead, Matza maintains that "most men, including delinquents, are neither wholly free nor completely constrained but fall somewhere between" (p. 27). The delinquent is not someone committed to deviant behavior, but neither is he one who, in complete freedom, chooses it. Rather his behavior is one of "drift"—that is, the delinquent is

> an actor neither compelled nor committed to deeds nor freely choosing them; neither different in any simple or fundamental sense from the law-abiding, nor the same; conforming to certain traditions in American life while partially unreceptive to other more conventional traditions; and finally, an actor whose motivational system may be explored along lines explicitly commended by classical criminology—his peculiar relation to legal institutions. (p. 28)

Most delinquents, Matza maintains, are drifters and do not become adult criminals. Having rejected the notion of delinquent subculture with its deterministic foundation, Matza essentially accepts the idea of subculture which "is of two minds regarding delinquency, one that allows members to behave illegally and to gain therefrom, the other reveals the impact of conventional precepts. Both frames of mind are necessary if we are to accurately portray the subculture of delinquency" (p. 40). Thus, to Matza, the subculture of delinquency is not the antithesis of the conventional culture; rather it

> consists of precepts and customs that are delicately balanced between convention and crime. The subculture posits objectives that may be attained through delinquency but also by other means. Its customs allow delinquency and even suggest it, but delinquency is neither demanded nor necessarily considered a preferred path. The norms and sentiments of the subculture are beliefs that function as the *extenuating conditions* under which delinquency is permissible. (p. 59)

The subculture provides for the legitimizing of the delinquent behavior by "techniques of neutralization" which consist of "obliterating the infractious nature of behavior. It converts infraction to mere action" (p. 176). Drift, arising from neutralization, does not guarantee delinquency; it "makes delinquency possible or permissible by temporarily removing the restraints that ordinarily control members of society" (p. 181). Whether the individual decides to commit the delinquency or not depends, in the final analysis, upon two conditions—one on "mundane occasions" and the other in "extraordinary situations" (pp. 183ff). In mundane or previously committed delinquencies, all that is required is adequate "preparation." For new experiences or extraordinary situations, there is required a feeling of "desperation," which results from a mood of fatalism.

Matza's reformulation of the subculture of delinquency, removing the determinism implicit in Cohen and Cloward and Ohlin and placing it in the context of drift, sharpens the basic difference between this approach and that of Miller. To Miller, again, delinquency is generated by lower class culture which differs in very basic ways from conventional middle class culture. To Matza, the delinquent shares the same values as the middle class, but drifts free from its constraint, at times, through the techniques of neutralization.

In summary then, we find that the bulk of delinquency theory can be separated into three strains: that which would deny any significant interrelation between poverty and crime; that which sees lower class crime as the result of structural constraints—situational adaptationalists (Merton, Thrasher, Cohen, Cloward and Ohlin, and Matza); and that which sees lower class delinquency as the direct product of lower class culture itself (Miller).

Insofar as Sutherland's critique of the data on crime is concerned, as was stated previously there is almost no criminologist who accepts the data at face value. Obviously they are biased to a great extent. However, this is insufficient grounds for dismissing any conclusions drawn from them because, as Cressey was quoted as saying in the section on crime in Chapter 1 of this volume, the evidence indicating a relationship between poverty and crime is so overwhelming that it would be stretching the point too far to assert that, because of inadequacies in recording procedures, the data are totally unreliable. Furthermore, the data derived from youth themselves likewise corroborate the higher incidence of delinquency among the lower class, as Reiss and Rhodes, and Clark and Wenninger found.[9] Finally, since the definition of crime is always social—that is, it is the society that defines certain acts as criminal—then the fact that there is an overrepresentation of persons in lower class in the reported crime data suggests that, at least among the crimes most "abhorred" (to use Durkheim's term) by the society, there is more of this activity in the lower class. While Sutherland is undoubtedly correct when he argues that many middle class persons commit white-collar crimes and that these rarely appear in the criminal statistics, the point is, however, that perhaps this should indicate that society does not consider white-collar crime as criminal as it does the crimes in which the lower class is most likely to engage. Among those crimes which most concern the society, however, there is an overrepresentation of persons in the lower class.

Walter B. Miller's contention that there is a distinct lower class culture and that it is this culture which is the generator of delinquency has been the source of a good deal of criticism. The basic question relates to the nature of this "lower class culture," which shall be explored in detail in the next chapter.

MENTAL ILLNESS

The structural or situational school argues that the higher rate of schizophrenia among persons in the lower class is the result of features in the lower class situation. The explanations in this school vary as to their identification of the specific features of the lower class situation which cause the higher incidence of schizophrenia. Thus, this school or perspective is basically situational in that it sees the schizophrenia arising out of the structural situation of poverty, and, in contrast to the previously discussed cultural approach, it is *realistic* rather than *nominalistic*, because it does accept the data as indicating a real problem of schizophrenia in the lower class. We shall not attempt to examine the variety of different explanations of the specifics of the lower class situation which cause schizophrenia; rather, only a few will be discussed and they may be taken as indications of the orientation of this approach.

John A. Clausen and Melvin Kohn (1959) conducted a survey of Hagerstown, Maryland, where they found no correlation between social class and schizophrenia. They therefore concluded that the relationship depends upon the size of the city. In a small town (Hagerstown), where there is integration between the social classes, there will be no correlation; only in larger cities (New York, Detroit) with social malintegration will there be an inverse relationship. Though Clausen and Kohn do not offer

---

[9]It should be noted that Travis Hirschi's (1969) study of juvenile delinquency, which was based on self-reported crime rather than on official records, found very little difference in rates by social class. However, in his review of the evidence, Jackson Toby suspects that the absence of a correlation between criminality and social class in the few self-report studies available, may well "be an artifact of the research procedures used in gathering the data" (Toby, 1974, p. 91).

the size of the city as the direct causal explanation, there seems to be some evidence from other studies that might help explain precisely in what way the size of the city has an effect on the rate of schizophrenia in the lower class of that city. John B. Calhoun (1963) conducted experiments on domesticated rats "for sixteen months in order to obtain detailed records of the modifications of behavior induced by population density" (p. 34), and his experiments showed that population density has clear consequences on the behavioral pathologies of the rats. He concludes

> that the behavioral repertory with which the Norway rat has emerged from the trials and errors of evolution and domestication must break down under the social pressures generated by population density. In time, refinement of experimental procedures and of the interpretation of these studies may advance our understanding to the point where they may contribute to the making of value judgments about analogous problems confronting the human species. (p. 43)

Recognizing that rats and human beings are distinct species and do not necessarily react in the same manner to the same situations and conditions, the results of Calhoun's experiments were thought to provide some leads for an understanding of the findings of Clausen and Kohn. Specifically, because the larger the city the more densely populated it will be, and because the lower class areas are invariably those with the greatest density of population, it has been suggested that the density reaches a point where it has an effect on the individuals in that area leading to a higher incidence of schizophrenia. Plausible as this idea may sound, recent studies by Jonathan L. Freedman (1973) indicate that it is untenable. Measuring density both in terms of number of people per square mile and number of people per room in a housing unit, Freedman found no more pathology in high-density areas than in low-density ones, when income and other factors are controlled (p. 61). Freedman concludes that density does intensify the effects of already existing negative social situations, but it does not create them. In fact, where positive social situations exist, "conditions of high density can have positive effects and need not have negative ones" (p. 121). The crucial variable is thus intensity of social interaction among residents, rather than the degree of population density.

We would like to offer one further step toward an explanation, along the above lines, based upon the reports of Abram Hoffer (1962), a Canadian psychiatrist, of success in treating certain forms of schizophrenia with injections of niacin. If this can be validated, and if, furthermore, it can be shown that certain forms of schizophrenia result from niacin deficiencies, the possibility exists that one source of the high rate of schizophrenia in the lower class is that the lower class is most likely to have the least nutritional diets and thus most likely to suffer from vitamin deficiency, specifically niacin deficiency, which may lead to schizophrenia. Further evidence along these lines, demonstrating the effects of nutritional deficiency, have been documented by William J. Culley (1965; abstract quoted in Hurley, 1969, p. 66):

> The nutritional aspects of mental retardation were reviewed. Two main categories were used: (1) nutritional deficiencies that cause mental retardation; and (2) nutritional problems associated with mental retardation. Some findings in the first category included: (1) caloric deficiency contributes to prematurity and greater incidence of mental retardation; (2) protein deficiency in pregnancy produces lower birth rates and less vitality in newborns; (3) a vitamin E deficient diet in pregnant rats causes encephaly in many of the young; (4) neuritis in animals is caused by a deficiency in thiamin (vitamin B1); (5) riboflavin (vitamin B2) deficiency in pregnant rats can cause CNS malformations (i.e., hydrocephalus); (6) niacin deficiency causes personality changes resembling psychoses and apathy; and (7) hydrocephaly has been produced in young whose mothers were on vitamin B12 deficient diets. The problems that would occur in the second category usually were due to motor disturbances in children leading to difficulty in chewing and swallowing food.

Given the effects of malnutrition on rats, it seems plausible that this condition may, in part, account for the high rate of schizophrenia among members of the lower classes in many cities. Furthermore, if this evidence of the effects on rats suggests anything insofar as similar effects upon human beings, it most certainly appears to negate the contention of the culturalists that the entire statistical relationship (or at least a good part of it) is due to psychiatric labeling and that the lower class manner of becoming ill (mentally) is no more severe than that of the middle class. The evidence which we have presented clearly indicates very deep and extensive effects produced by the situation of poverty.

There is a third type of explanation to the correlation between poverty and schizophrenia which we would like to look at briefly, primarily because it shows how to look at relationships critically and not accept them at their face value. This is the explanation known as the "drift hypothesis," according to which it is not poverty which causes schizophrenia, but rather it is the schizophrenia or the "pre-schizophrenia" which causes the individual suffering to "drift" into the lower class. One of the most recent versions of the drift hypothesis is that of Dunham (1965), who maintains that the concentration of schizophrenics in the lower class is the result of the competitive character of American society, and also the personality characteristics of the pre-schizophrenic who "is likely to suffer with respect to education and type of job," and is thus handicapped "in the competitive struggle which characterizes urban America" (p. 256). A follow-up study by Dunham (Dunham, Phillips, & Srinivasan, 1966) concludes that "it is the nature of the disease that determines the class position of the schizophrenic, at least by the measure of occupation and education, and that it is not the class position that influences the nature of the disease...Their premorbid personality characteristics prevent them from securing any position to which their education might entitle them; thus they are more likely to be counted as members of the lower class" (p. 226). Whereas Hollingshead and Redlich (1958), having investigated the residential histories of 428 patients, conclude that "schizophrenic patients committed to mental hospitals from slum areas do not drift there as an effect of their mental illnesses" (p. 246), Dunham et al. (1966) found that when they "worked out the social class position of the fathers and distributed the cases of schizophrenics in his sample by father's social class...the rates were at a parity in all five classes" (p. 233).

While it may be debatable insofar as the drift hypothesis is concerned, there is no question that the other explanations discussed in this chapter are of the situational version in that they posit the source of the high rate of schizophrenia among members of the lower class as arising out of features of the lower class situation.

EDUCATION

The problems confronted by children in the lower class with respect to education, particularly in the school, have been documented. In the previous chapter a series of explanations of these problems were discussed and the common thread running throughout was that the source of the problem lies somewhere in the different early primary socialization which the child in the lower class receives as compared to that of the middle class child. On the other hand, there is a very different approach—the situational one—which explains the source of the problems as lying in the inadequacies of the school system and in the negative attitude which that entire system has toward the lower class child. As Kenneth Clark (1967), among others, sees it, the problem is not one of cultural deprivation but *educational deprivation*:

> ...the cultural deprivation approach is seductive. It is both reasonable and consistent with contemporary environmentalistic thought, which seems to dominate social science thinking...To

> what extent are the contemporary social deprivation theories merely substituting notions of environmental immutability and fatalism for earlier notions of biologically determined educational unmodifiability? To what extent do all these theories obscure more basic reasons for the educational retardation of lower status children? To what extent do they offer acceptable and desired alibis for the educational default: the fact that these children, by and large, do not learn because they are not being taught effectively and they are not being taught because those who are charged with the responsibility of teaching them do not believe that they can learn, do not expect that they can learn, and do not act toward them in ways which help them to learn. (pp. 130-131)

Thus, to Clark, the source of the problem lies in the inadequacies of the school, and especially in the negative manner in which lower class children are viewed and related to in the school system.

Estelle Fuchs (1966) has found that, at least from the "definition of the situation" of the children involved, the problem lies within the school system. She reports that "not all children placidly accept the roles established for them by the school. Many suffer discomfort and acute distress from situations they view as denigrating their position to a continuation of lower-class, subordinate positions...From the point of view of the children interviewed...*the schools were seen as the source of their difficulty*" (pp. 142-143, emphasis added).

While we shall not get into a discussion of this matter at this point, it should be obvious that the approach one takes to remedying the problem of the lower class child in school would depend upon whether one takes a cultural or situational perspective as to its source: those who follow the cultural approach would emphasize compensatory education and cultural enrichment programs, whereas those who follow the situational approach would emphasize the changes necessary in teachers' attitudes, curricula, textbooks, etc. Many of the controversies in the area of urban or "inner city" education are essentially reflections of this basic difference in perspective between the culturalists and the situationalists.

FAMILY LIFE

Whereas Lee Rainwater (1960) found evidence to support the cultural perspective in the area of family planning, Frederick Jaffe and Steven Polgar (1968) report of their studies wherein the "findings support the hypothesis that the difficulties of the poor in family planning derive in very large measure from lack of realistic opportunities to achieve genuinely held aspirations for small families" (p. 229). This conclusion, it is fair to say, is representative of what may be termed a "strict stituationalist" perspective in that it leaves no room for the influence of values even in the sense in which Marx recognized values and ideologies as "false consciousness." To the strict situationalist, the social structure *overtly* restricts the possibilities open to the members of the lower class.

As was the procedure in the previous chapter, this chapter will conclude with a discussion of social policies which have derived from the situational perspective discussed.

An immediate derivative of Cloward and Ohlin's (1960) theory of lower class delinquency being related to lack of opportunity was the development of the Mobilization For Youth (MFY) project in New York City, which strove for opening up opportunities through on-the-job training, guidance and counseling, etc., for lower class youth. (Mobilization for Youth, 1961). It should be noted that this approach also follows logically from Merton's theory of "Social Structure and Anomie," which had so much influence upon Cloward and Ohlin. If the problem of lower class delinquency is seen as the result of restricted legitimate opportunities combined with their adherence to the dominant cultural goal of success—"making it"—then it follows that unless the goal is to be changed there must be an expansion of legitimate opportunities.

In the area of education, such innovations as decentralization, community control, open enrollment, and affirmative action are all based upon a situational perspective which defines the source of the problems of the poor in school as lying in the inadequacies and injustices of the existing structure.

Finally, for the present, if the higher birthrate of the poor is explained situationally, *a la* Jaffe and Polgar, then the activities of Planned Parenthood and the like should be directed, simply, to providing the poor with birth control information and devices. It was, for example, on the basis of this assumption that abortion reform was advocated in New York City and elsewhere.

Chapter 3

NEITHER STRUCTURAL NOR CULTURAL

From the late 1950s through the 1960s, the subject of poverty held a very prominent position in the research and literature of American sociology. To a considerable degree, this concentration on the subject of poverty was the result of the national concern with the problem of poverty and the proclamation by Congress and the President of a "War on Poverty." Sociologists and others thus began to look more closely at what was seen as *the* domestic problem of the country. Since it was a major social problem, as defined by the society, its government, and mass media, it quite naturally became a major area of focus for sociologists who specialized in the study of social problems. But, even more specifically, many social scientists hoped to be and were engaged by public and private poverty "warriors" as advisors and technicians for the purpose of devising and implementing "battle plans" in the war on poverty. The basic problem became, therefore, to explain the nature and reasons for the persistence of poverty in the United States and to develop programs for its eradication. As it turned out, most of the explanations of the persistence of poverty fell into the same categories which were used to explain the relationship between poverty and the variables which have been discussed in the preceding chapters—that is, poverty was explained as persisting due to either cultural—(internal) or situational—(external, structural) forces. As shall be demonstrated, neither of these positions accounts for the complete relationship between the poor and the non-poor in American society.

In 1959, Oscar Lewis coined the term "the culture of poverty" in an effort to explain the many similarities between lower class families in Mexico and those in other parts of the world. He subsequently elaborated upon that concept in a number of his writings and attempted thereby to explain the persistence of poverty in many countries. The basic idea did not originate with Oscar Lewis, as it has its roots in the Chicago School of Sociology and the work of Robert E. Park in particular. Park's formulation of the cultural perspective is seen in the following passage from "Human Behavior in Urban Environment" (Park & Burgess, 1925):

> The fact is... that the city is rooted in the habits and customs of the people who inhabit it. The consequence is that the city possesses a moral as well as a physical organization, and these two mutually interact in characteristic ways to mold and modify one another. It is the structure of the city which first impresses us by its visible vastness and complexity. But this structure has its basis, nevertheless, in human nature, of which it is an expression. On the other hand, *this vast organization which has arisen in response to the needs of its inhabitants, once formed, imposes itself upon them as a crude external fact, and forms them, in turn, in accordance with the design and interests which it incorporates.* (p. 4)

What Park says explicitly (and what is implicit in many of the works which derived from the Chicago school) is that the patterns of the neighborhood, and the slum in particular, once they come into being, take on a life of their own and are to a great extent self-generating and self-perpetuating.

Oscar Lewis, while not speaking about the same subject as Park, nevertheless implies a similar understanding in his earliest formulation of the notion of "the culture of poverty" as follows:

> ...poverty in modern nations...suggests class antagonisms, social problems, and the need for change; and it often is so interpreted by the subject of the study. Poverty has become a dynamic factor which affects participation in the larger national culture and creates a subculture of its own. One can speak of the culture of the poor, for it has its own modalities and distinctive social and psychological consequences for its members. It seems to me that the culture of poverty cuts across regional, rural-urban, and even national boundaries. For example, I am impressed by the remarkable similarities in family structure, the nature of kinship ties, the quality of husband-wife and parent-child relations, time orientation, spending patterns, value systems, and the sense of community found in lower-class settlements in London, in Puerto Rico, in Mexico City slums and Mexican villages, and among lower class Negroes in the United States. (1959, p. 16)

We must immediately clarify that when Lewis uses the term "culture of poverty" he actually means "subculture;" as he puts it: "While the term 'subculture of poverty' is technically more accurate, I have used 'culture of poverty' as a shorter form" (Lewis, 1966, p. xliii). Throughout our subsequent discussion it should be understood that the "culture" and "subculture" of poverty are used interchangeably.

The concept has been subjected to criticism on a variety of levels, and we shall examine each of these levels of criticism in order to determine the usefulness of the concept in understanding the persistence of poverty in the United States. We begin our analysis with one of the concept's major critics, Charles A. Valentine (1968), who rejects it on the grounds that poverty is situational, not cultural. We have seen these two positions in our discussions of the relationship between poverty and the variables discussed in our last three chapters, and it now behooves us to analyze the subject critically in order to arrive at any conclusions as to the applicability of the concept of subculture to the poor. This can only be accomplished after we have arrived at an understanding of the concept of subculture.

The term "subculture" is used much more frequently in the literature of sociology than in that of anthropology. Most sociologists who use the term do so as if its meaning were clearly understood—that is, they most often use the term without bothering to clearly define its meaning. There are a number of exceptions to this rule, and we shall now cite its usage and definition as found in the work of a number of anthropologists and sociologists. It is expected that this exercise will sharpen our understanding of the concept and clarify many of the misunderstandings involved in its usage.

Ralph Linton:

> While ethnologists have been accustomed to speak of tribes and nationalities as though they were the primary culture-bearing units, the total culture of a society is really an aggregate of subcultures. Within tribes or unmechanized civilizations these subcultures are normally carried by the various local groups which go to make the total society and are transmitted within these groups. In a few cases there may also be subcultures which are characteristic of particular social classes and which are transmitted within them, but this arrangement is much less characteristic than the local one. Every subculture always differs in some respects from all the rest, and the total culture consists of the sum of its subcultures plus certain additional elements which are a result of their interaction. (1936, p. 275)

Linton here points out two important features of subcultures: first, that they are the component parts of the total culture (that is, that a subculture is not to be thought of as a separate culture but rather a subsidiary unit within the larger national culture, and a unit of which that culture is composed); and secondly, that there are, at times, social classes that have their own subcultures.

Alfred Kroeber:

> We have seen how each class in a society exhibits a more or less distinct phase, a subculture, of the total culture carried by the society; just as geographical segments of the society manifest regional aspects of the culture. This principle extends farther; to age levels and sexes. Men do not practice the specific habits of the women in their culture, and vice versa. And though both sexes are generically oriented about these habits—they always know that certain peculiarly feminine (or masculine) activities exist—they may be so hazily informed about them that they could not adequately practice them or transmit them in their entirety if they would. At the same time these sex phases are never felt as constituting more than a side or an aspect of the culture—nor, indeed, do they constitute more.... The same thing holds, incidentally, for the class phases, and often for the regional phases, of well integrated cultures. Scavengers and bankers will be recognized in such cultures as quite properly following diverse strains of life and making diverse contributions, but their coherence within the body politic of culture and society is felt to outweigh their separateness. They are both organs within the same body, like the patricians and the plebians in the old Roman fable about the stomach and the limbs. (1948, p. 274)

Kroeber goes even further than did Linton in seeing that social classes may be thought of as subcultures (for a contrasting view of class, see Anderson, 1971, especially Chapter 3, "Classes in Industrial Society: Marxian Sociology," pp. 63-82), in that each of them has certain unique patterns or norms which distinguish it from the other social classes, yet, at the same time, each is part of a coherent whole. The following passages from Herskovits, Kluckhohn, and Gordon elaborate on this point.

Melville J. Herskovits:

> If we translate this [Sapir's discussion of linguistic drift—CIW] into terms of our discussion of variability in culture as a whole, we would say that the individual differences in belief and behavior of persons who belong to one sub-group or local community within a particular society are submerged in the consensus that characterize the subcultures of the two groups, and thus make it possible to distinguish them from each other in terms of their typical patterns of thought and conduct. (1948, p. 583)

Notice that here Herskovits speaks of the possibility of distinguishing subcultures on the basis of their "typical patterns of thought and conduct." This is crucial to our definition of subculture.

Clyde Kluckhohn:

> When one comes to the distinction between "language" and "dialect," the linguists have a rigorous criterion: If there is a mutual intelligibility, then they are dialects of the same language. I suggest that this should be a paradigm for our drawing the lines between "distinct cultures" and "subcultures of one culture." When people from two groups, despite perceptible variation in the details of their lifeways, nevertheless share enough basic assumptions so that they can communicate—comfortably, then their cultures are only variants of a single culture. (1962, p. 65)

Again, Kluckhohn emphasizes the difference between subcultures and separate cultures, and he applies a linguistic distinction as a means for differentiating between the two. We would argue that, within a larger national culture, as long as the one group does not consciously seek to separate itself from the larger culture in all respects, then it is still a subculture. The picture becomes clearer with the following by Milton M. Gordon:

> It is the thesis of this paper that a great deal could be gained by a more extensive use of the concept of *sub-culture*—a concept used here to refer to a subdivision of a national culture, composed of a combination of factorable social situations such as class status, ethnic background, regional and rural or urban residence, and religious affiliation, but *forming in their combination a functioning unity which has an integrated impact on the particular individual.* (1947, p. 40)

We are now in a position to define subculture as the culture of a subgroup within a larger society which may be distinguished from that larger society and the other groups of which it is composed on the basis of that subgroup's characteristic patterns of behavior, lifestyle, attitudes, and values. Thus, it is not uncommon to find in the literature on social stratification references to the term "class culture"; we have seen this in our discussion of Hollingshead, and we find the formulation as follows in a recent standard text on social stratification:

> We here use the concept of subculture to refer to a complex of interrelated learned beliefs, attitudes, values, and patterns of behavior common to a grouping within the larger society. These traits become generalized in symbols and thoughtways forming an ethos that reflects and is reflected by the details of group life. Most important, such traits are seized upon by other subgroups as bases for perceiving and acting toward members of the subculture, as determining their standing in the community, or as means to "hang people on their own peg." Some of the many class differences in subcultural "life style" recorded by research include differences in respect to type of residence, leisure and recreation, family life and ritual, church preference, sex mores and behavior, fashions, musical taste, drinking habits, and types of deviant behavior. (Mayer & Buckley, 1970, p. 55)

Before we pursue the concept of "class subculture," especially insofar as it relates to the lower class, we must say a few more words about our definition of subculture. The question may well be asked: to what extent must the patterns of behavior, attitudes, and values of a particular group be unique in order for it to qualify as a subculture under our definition? Regretfully, we can supply no exact answer. There is, admittedly, a degree of imprecision in our formulation of the concept of subculture; however, this is not unique in the vocabulary of the social sciences. All that can be expected is that the concept will be as precise as possible; a degree of imprecision must be expected owing to the nature of that which is being analyzed. We even find a similar situation with the concept of class in social stratification. Gerhard Lenski (1966) writes:

> Whether we like it or not, this kind of phrasing is forced on us by the nature of the reality we seek to analyze. In most cases human populations simply are not stratified into a limited number of clearly differentiated, highly discrete categories. Rather, they tend to be strung out along continua which lack breaks that can be utilized as class boundaries. Furthermore, if we were to insist that members of classes stand in identical positions with respect to the distribution of things of value, we should have thousands, possibly millions, of classes in many societies, most with but a handful of members, and some with only one. To avoid this, we are forced to use less restrictive criteria, but this forces us to use less *precise* ones. In general, students of stratification have found it more advantageous to employ a smaller number of larger and more inclusive classes....The use of such categories isn't meant to deny the exis-

> tence of internal variation within these classes. Obviously each class can be subdivided into more homogeneous subcategories or subclasses....The extent to which this is done depends largely on the nature of the study. (pp. 76-77)

A similar situation also exists with reference to the concept of "race." If one's objective is to demonstrate differences among human beings, one may conceive of anywhere from two to more than 200 races, depending on one's criteria; if the objective is to demonstrate similarities among human beings, one may, as anthropologist Morton Fried does, abandon the concept completely, since the physical similarities among human beings outnumber the differences along the order of 95 to 5 (*Time*, 1967).

Finally, Marvin Harris (1964) makes the same point in his discussion of the social and cultural:

> In this usage, society denotes the population whose behavior stream is the object of study. Since there are no perfectly isolated human populations, the boundaries of a given society may fluctuate according to the nature of the observer's research interests. Hence, one may speak of the society of a primitive village or tribe, the society of a small town in the United States, the society of the town and its hinterland, the society of the whole country, Western society, or the society of all mankind. (pp. 182-183)

Thus, if one's frame of reference is the poor or the lower class in the United States, one may single them out for analysis in terms of their characteristic norms and attitudes. This is the sense in which the concept of subculture has been applied to the poor. Of course, it yet remains for us to determine that the poor are, in fact, characterized by unique patterns of behavior and attitudes. For the present, we are merely indicating the framework within which the concept of "the culture of poverty" operates. Furthermore, we shall see later that the mere isolating of the poor for analysis under this framework has its own effects.

Let us, rather, return to the concept of subculture and see if we can specify a number or variety of different types of subcultures. We should emphasize that the types which we identify should be understood as being "ideal types," with degrees of variation within each category and possible overlap between categories. Again, it is not our objective to derive a rigorous typology of subcultures, but merely to point out some of their more salient features in order that we may be in a better position to critically analyze its formulation in the context of the culture of poverty.

One type, which we may term "normative" subcultures, is likely to arise as the society moves from quite primitive, simple stages to more complex stages, so that there develops greater social differentiation in education, occupation, residence, etc. This is, basically, the type of subculture to which Kroeber alluded in our earlier discussion in this chapter. The more complex the society becomes, the more it is likely that each group will be less familiar with all aspects of other groups in the society. In the area of occupation, for example, specialization develops; as a result, each group of specialists in a particular field shares in its specialty and, simultaneously, in its unfamiliarity with other specialties. Specialization serves as the basis for ingroup formation and maintenance because as each individual becomes more involved with his own specialty, he will become increasingly less familiar with others in other specialties. Thus, in American society we may speak of a subculture of intellectuals.[10] That they are so perceived can be deduced from former Vice President Spiro T. Agnew's characterization of them as "an effete corps of impudent snobs who characterize themselves as intellectuals."[11] Similarly, Albert J. Reiss, Jr. (1971, pp. 121-172) has presented a vivid portrait of the police subculture.

Minority subcultures would be those whose unique norms and values are considered legitimate by the society at large, despite the fact that they are different from the dominant ones. An example of this type of subculture is an ethnic group that migrates to the society or is incorporated into the society as the result of geographic expansion. Such a subculture would persist from the time that the acculturation process begins and until such time as it becomes fully assimilated into the dominant culture. This subculture may persist voluntarily because its members desire to perpetuate its unique lifestyles, as in the case of some religious and ethnic subcultures, or it may persist as the result of social barriers imposed upon it by the dominant society, prohibiting its complete assimilation into the dominant culture, as in the case of other religious and ethnic minorities. Most often, it will persist because of both internal and external reasons. In some instances, the internal pressures will lead to external barriers being superimposed upon them, and in other instances the continued external social barriers may lead to internal pressures toward degrees of separatism. Black nationalism would be an example of the latter situation.

In the area of deviant subcultures, we can identify three types, analogous to three of Robert K. Merton's "Modes of Adaptation" (1938, p. 676). Merton identifies "Innovation" (II) as characteristic of those who deviate from the institutionalized means in their attempt to attain the culture goals; "Retreatism" (IV), of those who adhere to neither the

---

[10] See Edward Shils, "The Intellectual and the Powers: Some Perspectives for Comparative Analysis," in Rieff (1970), pp. 27-51. See especially the sections on "The Structure of the Intellectual Community," pp. 35-42, and "The Traditions of Intellectuals," pp. 42-51.

[11] Quoted in *Congressional Quarterly,* Nov. 14, 1969, p. 2279.

institutionalized means nor the culture goals; and "Rebellion" (V), of those who denounce both the means and the goals. In adopting parts of Merton's typology, we shall modify the focus from modes of individual adaptation (pertaining to the isolated individual) to modes of group adaptation (pertaining to individuals within groups of similar individuals). Thus, the mode of adaptation is not simply an individual characteristic, but rather is characteristic of groups.

Classes II and IV, by virtue of their nonconformance with the institutionalized means, would both be deviant subcultures, the difference between them being that Class II, "Innovation," is deviant insofar as the means utilized in the attainment of the culture goals, whereas Class IV, "Retreatism," is deviant not only insofar as means but also as it deviates from the culturally prescribed goals.

There is much discussion in the literature concerning the goals of delinquent gangs, as we have already seen in Chapter 2. For the present, we would consider white-collar criminality as an example of the innovative subculture, for in this case the members of the group are utilizing what the dominant legal system regards as deviant means to achieve the cultural goals. (The term "innovative" is used here as Merton does, to refer to means.)

Our second class of deviant subcultures, "Retreatism," would apply to the groups Merton (1938) refers to: "psychotics, autists, pariahs, outcasts, vagrants, vagabonds, tramps, chronic drunkards and drug addicts" (p. 677). That these groups do form a subculture or subcultures has been well documented by Samuel E. Wallace (1968), who concludes that "the skid row way of life with its prescribed ways of behavior toward members and non-members, with its institutions, socialization, status order, special language, and tradition is a subculture" (p. 141).

Class V, the rebellious subculture, refers to those groups that deviate from the institutional means and culture goals and have, or are trying to, set up an alternative set of means and goals. They have a positive commitment to "a new way of life," to a "counter culture" (see Roszak, 1969). This would apply most commonly in contemporary American society to some of the politically active hippie groups and to some of the groups of extreme political radicals of the late 1960s, such as the Weatherman faction of the Students for a Democratic Society (SDS) and, possibly, to the Black Panthers.

Having looked at a variety of different groups which may be characterized as subcultures, we are now in a better position to understand what is meant when the poor are characterized as a subculture. This means, at the very least, that the poor may be distinguished from the rest of the society and characterized on the basis of certain unique qualities or features. Now, as we mentioned earlier, Charles A. Valentine maintains that the behavioral patterns of the poor are not cultural, but rather merely situational. That is, they are not patterns that have been internalized and become part of the traditions of the group, the "recipes for living," but rather are merely external modes of adaptation which would readily be abandoned under different conditions. To a great extent, this criticism involves the question of the attitudes and values of the poor and whether or not they are different from those of the non-poor; that is a matter to which we shall turn later in this chapter. For the moment, let us examine more closely this distinction which Valentine makes between cultural patterns and situational adaptations, a matter which has been running through almost all of our analysis thus far.

Deriving from the concern of many anthropologists with primitive and strongly tradition-oriented societies, there has evolved the notion that the traditional, intergenerationally transmitted factor is an essential component of culture. A pattern is cultural, it is maintained, only if this tradition element is present. Culture, accordingly, must involve at least two generations. Otherwise, a pattern is but a situational adaptation, not a cultural one. Cultural patterns are those that have been passed on intergenerationally as part of the way things are done, the "recipes for living," whereas situational adaptations are merely immediate responses to particular circumstances and disappear when the particular circumstance changes. The situational adaptation, therefore, is but a short-lived response to an external situation; it is not internalized. If, however, this pattern, which began as a situational adaptation, does become transmitted over generations—does take on the authority of tradition—then it can be said to have evolved into a cultural pattern. William Graham Sumner (1959) describes the process in his discussion of the origin of folkways:

> Men begin with acts....Need was the first experience, and it was followed at once by a blundering effort to satisfy it....Thus ways of doing things were selected, which were expedient. They answered the purpose better than other ways, or with less toil and pain. Along the course on which efforts were compelled to go, habit, routine, and skill were developed. The struggle to maintain existence was carried on, not individually, but in groups. Each profited by the other's experience; hence there was concurrence towards that which proved to be most expedient. All at last adopted the same way for the same purpose; hence the ways turned into customs and became mass phenomena....The young learn them by tradition, imitation, and authority. (p. 2)

It is at that point that they are learned by tradition, imitation, and authority that they become cultural; prior to that point, they are *situational.*

While it is readily understandable that this distinction between the cultural and the situational should arise, as we noted, due to the concentration of anthropologists upon very stable societies, the experience in developing and modern societies demonstrates quite conclusively that this distinction is not always warranted or applicable. As Marvin Harris (1964) has noted:

> The emphasis which anthropologists have placed upon intergenerational continuity of response repertory is responsible for a great deal of confusion in the social sciences. When culture is defined in conformity with this emphasis, it attracts the merited scorn of sociologists for its evident failure to embrace some of the most interesting phenomena in modern industrial society. If culture consists only of cross-generationally duplicated responses, what is one to call those episodes, scenes, and groups which are newly arisen in the cauldron of industrial innovation? A concept which emphasizes the ageless traditions lazily yielding to the gentle pressure of change may profitably be applied to the Arunta or the Mohave...but it is certainly incongruous in the twentieth century. (p. 176)

Modern industrial society and the phenomenon of rapid social change is evidence that there can be cultural patterns which lack the element of intergenerational continuity and tradition. Conversely, in terms of our subject, some cultural patterns with long traditions may rapidly disappear with the advent of industrialization. As George P. Murdock (1969) puts it:

> Ethnography demonstrates that, when faced with expanded possibilities of cultural choice, all people reveal a preference for steel over stone axes, for quinine and penicillin over magical therapy, for money over barter, for animal and vehicular transport over human porterage, for improvement in the food supply which enable them to rear their children and support their aged rather than killing them, and so on. They relinquish cannibalism and headhunting with little resistance when colonial governments demonstrate the material advantages of peace. (p. 149)

What emerges, therefore, is the realization that cultural patterns and situational adaptations are not necessarily contradictory; rather, we see that many patterns become cultural precisely because of their adaptive quality. Lacking any alternatives, real or perceived, these patterns may become "the way things are done" *under these circumstances!* The intergenerational transmission aspect of culture refers not to the conditions but to the patterns of adapting to these conditions.

The failure to recognize the adaptive quality of culture and the failure to analytically distinguish between the situation, per se, and the modes of adapting to the situation, has been the source of a mass of confusion and logically unfounded criticisms on the subject of "the culture of poverty." Thus, for example, we find Lewis Coser (1968) arguing:

> The notion of culture implies the notion of a desired and highly valued way of life. It is rooted in the idea that men belonging to a culture are devoted to it and give it their loyalty because it embodies for them prized qualities and valued virtues. But how can a "culture of poverty" be valued and desired? Poverty is not a positive virtue. It is, instead, a negative condition, that one wishes to escape.... Their status is marked only by negative attitudes, that is, by what these status-holders do *not* have. If this is the case, then the whole notion of a culture of poverty is inherently untenable. (p. 270)

There are at least three fallacies in this criticism. First of all, while doubtlessly unintended, it manifests either historical ignorance or a form of ethnocentrism that sees the contemporary American condition as *the* norm. For the fact of the matter is that in some societies poverty has been a positive virtue, not "a negative condition, that one wishes to escape." As E. V. Walter (1970) has shown:

> Being poor has not always implied emotional depression and low aspiration—for the early Christians, the highest optimism and spiritual aspirations were reserved for the poor. Being poor has not always meant low status and low self-esteem—for the post-exilic Hebrews and the early Christians, the poor were the faithful remnant, beloved by God, and "the saints." Being poor has not always implied isolation and absence of community—the medieval poverty movement was marked by great solidarity in communities of the poor. (p. 4)

In fact, Oscar Lewis (1966) himself makes this very point when he distinguishes between poverty and the culture of poverty:

> There are degrees of poverty and many kinds of poor people. The culture of poverty refers to one way of life shared by poor people in given historical and social contexts.... There are a number

> of historical examples of very poor segments of the population which do not have a way of life which I would describe as a subculture of poverty. (p. xlviii)

So, our first criticism is of Coser's very biased view of the poor.

Secondly, Coser has somehow seen fit to ignore the emphasis of a number of writers who show that there are in fact positive qualities in the culture of poverty. Again, Lewis (1966) was very explicit on this:

> Middle-class people, and this would certainly include most social scientists, tend to concentrate on the negative aspects of the culture of poverty. They tend to associate negative valences to such traits as present-time orientation and concrete versus abstract orientation. I do not intend to idealize or romanticize the culture of poverty. As someone has said, "It is easier to praise poverty than to live in it;" yet some of the positive aspects which may flow from these traits must not be overlooked. (p. li)

And, Frank Riessman wrote his book, *The Culturally Deprived Child* (1962) for the expressed purpose of developing "new approaches to underprivileged [sic] individuals by emphasizing the positive aspects of their cultures which, hitherto, have been largely ignored" (p. xiii).

Finally, Coser falls victim to the very fallacy which he attributes to the culture of poverty theorists. Certainly, to the middle class observer, the culture of poverty is marked by negative attitudes. Certainly, to someone who is aware of and can achieve alternative conditions, there is no desire to be poor. But what is at question is the very recognition and aspiration for possible alternatives. We have previously cited Murdock, who has shown that, when faced with realistically perceived alternatives, people may quickly abandon cultural patterns which have long traditions. As long as these patterns (which their rapid abandonment proves are "negative") are maintained, however, because of the lack of perceived alternatives, they may certainly be cultural.

Having demonstrated that there is no necessary contradistinction between cultural patterns and situational adaptations—on the contrary, as we have seen, patterns may become cultural precisely because of their situational quality—we now come to one of the more basic questions, which deals with the values of the poor. We have already seen that on the basis of patterns of behavior there is a lower class lifestyle. The question now is whether, in addition to patterns of behavior, the poor may be distinguished on the basis of a uniquely lower class value system, or whether they adhere to the dominant middle class value system and only behave differently because of their economic situation. To put it another way, the question is whether there is, in fact, a real subculture of poverty, including not only norms but attitudes and values, or whether there is merely a poverty lifestyle, involving only patterns of behavior which develop solely because of their adaptational value.

Among those who would deny a uniquely lower class value system, we have previously cited the conclusions of Jaffe and Polgar in the area of family planning, who maintain that the poor hold the same aspirations for small families as do the non-poor, but fail in this because of the "lack of realistic opportunities to achieve" the genuinely held aspirations.

Hylan Lewis (1976), in his research on mother-headed Negro families in Washington, D.C. reports:

> The evidence suggests that Negro mothers from the low-income category, as much as any mother in any category of our population, want and prefer their men to be strong and supportive in marriage, family, and community relationships. There is no need to invoke a mystique of matriarchy to explain low-income, female-headed child-rearing units when we take into consideration the economic pressures of late twentieth-century urban living upon the young adult Negro male, and especially the ways in which these alter the choices open to low-income women and men....(p. 158)
>
> The behavior of the bulk of poor Negro families appears as pragmatic adjustments to external and internal stresses and deprivations experienced in the quest for essentially common values. (p. 170)

Similarly, Elliot Liebow (1967), in his study of Negro streetcorner men in Washington, D.C. concludes that

> ...the streetcorner man does not appear as a carrier of an independent cultural tradition. His behavior appears not so much as a way of realizing the distinctive goals and values of his own subculture, or of conforming to its models, but rather as his way of trying to achieve many of the goals and values of the larger society, of failing to do this, and of concealing this failure from others and from himself as best he can. (p. 222)

Charles S. Johnson was voicing this same position when he wrote, in 1941, of lower class Negro youth: *"They may be sensitive to community values* but forced to live only as conditions permit" (1967, p. 99, emphasis added).

Basically, all of these are echoing the common American value system view of Robert Merton (1938), who maintains that in American society, "the actual social organization is such that there exist class differentials in the accessibility of these *common* success symbols" (p. 680).

On the other hand, Walter B. Miller, Lee Rainwater, Oscar Lewis, and others see the lower class as possessing a distinctive value system. We thus have two contradictory views on the question of lower class values: one group of theorists sees the poor as sharing in the dominant values but forced to behave differently because of their economic situation, and one group of theorists sees a uniquely lower class value system.

William L. Yancey (1965) attributes the conflict between these two theoretical positions to the nature of the research upon which the theorist has relied. Those postulating a common value system have relied upon secondary materials, stemming stereotypically from the Durkheimian tradition, oriented toward the entire society and the dominant value structure. Those postulating a class differentiated value system—the earliest being those in the Chicago School—have relied upon ethnographic research stemming from "the Marxian tradition with its sympathetic orientation toward the lower classes [and thus] see subcultural values as developing directly out of the environment, with little or no attention being placed on their relationship to the larger society" (pp. 10-11).

We would disagree with Yancey for several reasons. First of all, the recent ethnographically oriented studies that were just discussed of, for example, Hylan Lewis and Elliot Liebow conclude that the poor do share in the dominant value structure. Moreover, we are not as certain as Yancey of what a Marxian tradition would conclude on the question of lower class values, and we are not convinced of the Marxian sympathetic attitude toward the poor. Actually, it would seem to depend upon whether "the poor" or "the lower class" in most of the studies with which we have been dealing is comparable with the "*Proletariat*" or the "*Lumpenproletariat*" of Marx. If what we are dealing with is what Marx referred to as "*Lumpenproletariat,*" then Yancey is quite incorrect when he attributes a sympathetic orientation in Marx toward this group. On the contrary, Marx and his followers despised this group almost as much as, if not more than, the "*Bourgeoisie.*" For example, in the *Manifesto of the Communist Party*, Marx and Engels had the following to say about it:

> The "dangerous class," the social scum, that passively rotting mass thrown off by the lowest layers of old society, may, here and there, be swept into the movement by a proletarian revolution; its conditions of life, however, prepare it far more for the part of a bribed tool of reactionary intrigue. (Feuer, 1959, p. 18)

As for the question of dominant value structure, a Marxian orientation should lead to the opposite conclusion than that which Yancey maintains it does, for Marx saw the poor as being exploited. Since everything flows from one's economic condition or situation according to Marx, then the behavior of the poor must be no more than a situational adaptation to an economically inferior position. It is from this very orientation that Eleanor B. Leacock (1967) accuses American social scientists of presenting a distorted image of the working class because almost all of their writings "contribute in one way or another to the picture of a people who, lacking family organization and reared without consistent and close relations, so the argument runs, are passive, have difficulty with abstract thinking and communication, seek escape from problems through relatively uninhibited expressions of sex or aggression, lack ego strength and are unable to plan for the future" (p. 3). She rejects this portrait, sees the behavior of the poor solely "as a specific response to social and economic realities" (p. 3), and bemoans that "one observes the mundane and unimaginative conformity that leads social scientists to confuse and distort reality. One witnesses colleagues, whom one knew as rebellious students interested in Marxist theory, adapting ideas borrowed therefrom to prevailing modes of discourse, in keeping with the advance of personal careers" (p. 5). While we would take strong issue with much of what Leacock has to say in that article, she is quite correct that a strictly Marxian analysis would insist upon a situational, rather than cultural, interpretation.

Despite our disagreement with Yancey on the aforementioned grounds, we would agree with him that most of those postulating a common value system have relied upon presumptions and secondary materials, for when we examine the few empirical studies available on the subject of values, the evidence seems to indicate (though not conclusively, as we shall see) that the poor do indeed differ somewhat in terms of values from the non-poor. As we shall further see, however, this does not completely resolve our problem.

One of the earliest empirical studies of the values of the poor as compared to those of the non-poor was that of Herbert H. Hyman (1953), and was an effort to determine whether or not members of the lower class hold to certain beliefs and values that are different from those of the middle class, and, whether or not these different beliefs and values, if they do exist, contribute in and of themselves to the perpetuation of one's membership in the lower class. His hypothesis was "that an intervening variable mediating the relationship between low position and lack of upward mobility is a system of beliefs and values within the lower classes which in turn reduces the very voluntary actions which would ameliorate their low position" (p. 427). Granting that values are only one of the variables which determine an individual's position in the social hierarchy, and indeed some of the determinants might be beyond the control of even the most highly motivated individual, Hyman maintains that, "however, within the bounds of the freedom available to individuals, this value system would create a *self-imposed* barrier to an improved position (p. 427). From data collected in a number of public opinion surveys, Hyman demonstrates that the lower class places less value on higher education (pp. 429-432), and that "the lower class individual holds values of such a nature as to reduce his striving towards those ends which would result in his moving up the class structure" (p. 432—namely, the lower class individual strives less for success, is aware of lack of opportunity, and does not value education (pp. 432-438). Then Hyman raises the question of whether perhaps "the person really wants to achieve the goal of great success, but that he merely accommodated himself to his lesser opportunities and reduced his aspirations so as to guard against the experience of frustration and failure" (p. 438). This is basically the position of Liebow (1967), who maintains that "increasingly he (the lower class Negro) turns to the streetcorner where a shadow system of values constructed out of public fictions serves to accommodate just such men as he, permitting them to be men once again provided they do not look too closely at one another's credentials" (p. 213). In a footnote to the above, Liebow declares that the values of the shadow system "are derivative, subsidiary in nature, thinner and less weighty, less completely internalized and seem to be value images reflected by forced or adaptive behavior rather than real values with a positive determining influence on behavior of choice" (p. 213). Hyman rejects this interpretation on the grounds that "the fact that the data for the sample of youth parallel so closely the findings on adults suggests that this explanation is not generally tenable. Such a dynamic readjustment of goals in relation to reality would be expected to come later. Youth seem to have internalized differentiated goals dependent on their class at an age too early to represent a kind of secondary re-setting of their sights" (1953, p. 438).

Bernard C. Rosen (1956) conducted a study of male high school sophomores in New Haven, designed to test the hypothesis that social classes differ in achievement motivation (Murray's "need achievement") "which provides internal impetus to excel," and "value orientations which define and implement achievement motivated behavior" (p. 204). Rosen further hypothesized that the incidence of both achievement motivation and values "is greater among persons of the middle class than those in the lower class" (p. 204). His results "support the hypothesis that social strata differ from one another in the degree to which the achievement motive is characteristic of their members. Furthermore, the data indicate that members of the middle class have considerably higher need achievement scores than individuals in the lower social strata" (pp. 205-206). Finally, for our purposes, "an analysis of the data supports the hypothesis that the middle class is characterized by a larger proportion of persons with achievement oriented values than are the lower social strata" (p. 208).

In another study by Rosen (1959), examining the differences in motivation and values of six racial and ethnic groups, he found that "ethnic differences persist when social class is controlled, but *some of the differences between ethnic groups in motivation, values, and aspirations are probably also a function of their class composition*" (p. 60, emphasis added).

There have been several interesting attempts to reinterpret the data and thereby synthesize the two conflicting positions. Hyman Rodman (1963) has suggested that there exists a "Lower Class Value Stretch" according to which

> ...the lower class person, without abandoning the general values of the society, develops an alternative set of values. Without abandoning the values of marriage and legitimate childbirth he stretches these values so that a non-legal union and legally illegitimate children are also desirable. The result is that the members of the lower class, in many areas, have a wider range of values than others within the society. They share the general values of the society with members of other classes, but in addition they have stretched these values, or developed alternative values, which help them to adjust to their deprived circumstances. (p. 209)

It should be noted that the value stretch is not quite the same as the "techniques of neutralization" discussed above by Matza (1964). Rodman (Rodman & Grams, 1967) distinguishes between himself and Matza in that "Matza suggests that delinquents have stretched the range of extenuating circumstances which excuse a delinquent act while retaining the conventional values. Rodman suggests that lower class individuals have stretched their range of values to include uniquely lower class values while retaining the conventional values" (p. 193).

In terms of our problem, Rodman (1966) states: "those who suggest that members of the lower class reject the dominant values and develop alternative values seem from our data to be wrong. Those who suggest that members of the lower class share the dominant values and reject alternative values, also seem to be wrong." In fact, he maintains, "many members of the lower class share the dominant values and have also stretched these values and developed a set of values unique to themselves" (p. 683).

Regarding studies, such as that of Hyman, which conclude that there are uniquely lower class beliefs and values, Rodman maintains that they are methodologically inconclusive:

> When a subject is asked for a single "value" (or norm, aspiration, goal) response among a number of alternatives, and he selects a single alternative, this cannot be taken as evidence that he holds only the selected value and no other values. Regardless of the care taken in constructing a questionnaire, value alternatives that are mutually exclusive in a psychological sense cannot be set up. (1963, p. 207)

We shall soon see that there are possibilities in questionnaire constructing which Rodman did not consider and which lead to a different conclusion. But first let us look at one more attempt at synthesizing the two positions on values.

Wan Sang Han (1969) has attempted to reconcile the two conflicting positions by distinguishing between wishes and expectations:

> When adolescents' wishes and expectations with respect to their future achievement are sharply discriminated, their SELW (socioeconomic level of wish) tends to transcend their awareness of restricted opportunities and ability in the pursuit of success goals. On the other hand, SELE (socioeconomic level of expectation) is significantly affected by limitations–perceptions. Thus, if any assertion concerning success is made in terms of SELW (or simply wishes), the view of common values seems valid while the position of class differential values seems tenable when an interpretation is made in terms of SELE (or simply expectations). (p. 688)

In other words, Han maintains that the common values position is correct in terms of wishes, in that the lower class would like to achieve the same goals as those of the middle class, whereas the class differential (or differentiated) values position is correct in that the lower class doesn't expect to achieve the same goals as does the middle class.

Intriguing as these two attempts at reconciliation appear, we find them both inconclusive. As far as Han's distinction between wishes and expectations, we would assert that if those wishes which he maintains are the same as those of the middle class are of any relevance, they are so only insofar as they affect the behavior of those who hold them. That is, what we are concerned with is values which affect action; otherwise, those wishes would be in the category of fantasy. So long as those wishes are completely devoid of any element of expectation, they are irrelevant to our subject, and all we can consider are "expectations" or SELE; insofar as these are concerned, Han finds agreement with the class differentiated values position.

As for Rodman, we agree with him that when a questionnaire asks the respondent to select a single value response among a number of alternatives, it is inconclusive. However, there is another method, which has been devised by Milton Rokeach and Seymour Parker (1970), that does appear to be quite reliable. Rokeach and Parker had a Value Survey administered by the National Opinion Research Center in April 1968 to 1400 Americans over 21 years of age, in an attempt to determine the usefulness of values as social indicators specifically with respect to the questions of the existence of a "culture of poverty" and a "Black culture" in America. Using the Rokeach Value Survey, consisting of a set of 18 "terminal" values—"preferred end-states of existence that people strive for"—and a set of 18 "instrumental" values—"preferred modes of behavior"—with each set arranged in alphabetical order, they asked each respondent to rearrange each set of 18 values in order of importance as "guiding principles in your daily life" (p. 97). The responses were then broken down by income into seven income groups, by education into seven educational levels, and by race into white and black. The results showed that insofar as income is concerned, "nine of the eighteen terminal values, and eleven of the eighteen instrumental values show significant differences associated with being poor or rich" and, therefore, "the many differences found between the poor and the rich on terminal and instrumental values suggest that these groups are characterized by profoundly different value systems and may be regarded as subculturally distinct" (p. 103). Rokeach and Parker note, however, that the differences between the poor and the non-poor "are not to be thought of in a dichotomous way, but in terms of a continuum of status" (p. 103). Thus, while their data seem to validate the existence of a culture or subculture of poverty, it should be clear that it exists not in relation to a "culture of the non-poor" but only in relation to a range of class cultures, such as "working class culture," "middle class culture," and "upper class culture." It is, however, most different from the "normative" culture.[12]

The Rokeach-Parker study refutes the conclusion of Han in that their "terminal values" would appear to reflect "wishes" rather than "expectations," and yet they found significant differences even on those between the poor and the upper classes. Insofar as the value stretch, Rokeach and Parker have accounted for Rodman's criticism of Hyman in that the respondent was not asked to select a single alternative, but rather to rank the values in order of the importance which he attaches to them.

[12] Though it doesn't bear directly on our topic, we feel it significant that Rokeach and Parker (1970) found socio-economic status to be a much more important indicator of values than race. "When status is held constant, or when poor whites and Negroes are compared with one another, most of the differences disappear" (p. 111).

As Rokeach and Parker state, they "have proceeded on the assumption that men do not differ from one another so much in whether or not they possess certain values, but rather in how they pattern them and rank them in order of importance" (p. 98).

As we said earlier, however, even this does not resolve our basic problem as to the cause of the persistence of poverty. While we are in a position to conclude that there is a subculture of poverty (that is, the poor may be distinguished on the basis of unique patterns of behavior and priorities of values), what we are still left with is the question as to whether that "culture of poverty" is the cause, as the culturalists maintain, or the result, as some situationalists might maintain, of the persistence of poverty. One cannot, for example, make any conclusions from the Rokeach and Parker study as to whether the lower class values, or their rank order, are the source of the culture of poverty or are merely the result of low economic position. The distinction between "subculture" as an explanatory concept and as a descriptive concept was raised in Matza's (1964) criticism of its usage in the sociological explanation of gang delinquency. He maintains that "there is a subculture of delinquency, but it is not a delinquent subculture" (p. 33), by which he means that the gangs do form subcultures, but that their delinquent acts cannot be explained as being determined by that subculture. Among the culture of poverty theorists, however, the implicit (and sometimes, explicit) assertion is that the persistence of poverty can be subculturally explained.

Oscar Lewis (1966), for example, maintains that it is the culture of poverty which generates poverty—that is, the culture of poverty is *self-perpetuating*: "By the time slum children are age six or seven they have usually absorbed the basic values and attitudes of their subculture and are not psychologically geared to take full advantage of changing conditions or increased opportunities which may occur in their lifetime" (p. liv).

Walter B. Miller (1958) is even more explicit when he states that "there is a substantial segment of present-day American society whose way of life, values, and characteristic patterns of behavior are the *product* of a distinctive cultural system which may be termed lower class....Lower class culture is a distinctive tradition many centuries old with an integrity of its own" (p. 19).

Whereas, on the basis of the evidence presented, we must reject the situational perspective which maintains that the only thing the poor share as compared to the non-poor is their economic situation, that the whole notion of a culture of poverty is completely untenable, we also cannot accept the cultural perspective which explains the persistence of poverty as being solely the product of the culture of poverty, and which sees that culture of poverty as completely distinctive and isolated from the dominant culture. First of all, there is no empirical evidence to support this position, and secondly and more importantly it seems to be irreconcilable with at least Oscar Lewis' assertion that the culture of poverty is more likely to develop in class-stratified, capitalistic societies than in socialistic ones such as Cuba. If the nature of the distributive system is a variable in the development of the culture of poverty, then it would appear to be implausible to suggest that the culture of poverty exists in isolation, or completely independently of the dominant culture.

It should be emphasized that both the cultural and situational perspectives which have just been discussed are extreme positions and that there are both culturalists and situationalists of varying degrees who would accept neither of these extremes. However, as the tempo of the argument rose, especially during the 1960s, due to the perceived policy implications of each position, what emerged was a debate so emotionally charged that it presented only an "either-or" situation; either one was a staunch culturalist or a staunch situationalist (see Waxman, 1970).

In contrast with each of these positions, it is the argument of this work that the "culture of poverty"—that is, the cluster of traits significantly related to lower class status in the United States—is neither cultural nor situational. This cluster exists and persists neither for solely internal nor for solely external reasons or sources. Even if it were conceded that Yancey (1965) is correct, we would argue that it was neither Durkheim nor Marx but Max Weber who provided the conceptual framework within which we can more adequately understand the lower class style of life. According to Weber (1968), structured social inequality involves, in addition to economic stratification, what he terms "status groups," the important elements of which are "status honor," "style of life," and "restrictions on social intercourse" (Vol. 2, p. 932). In the case of the positive status groups, the restrictions on social intercourse are internally derived for the purpose of protecting the position of that positive status group. In the case of the negative status group, which Weber terms the "negatively privileged status group" (p. 934), the restrictions would invariably come from without the group, from the higher status group. If the lower class in American society is a negative status group and there are restrictions on social intercourse, as will be demonstrated, then it should be apparent that to account for the cluster of traits composing the "culture of poverty," neither the cultural nor the situational explanations will suffice; they are, by virtue of the lower class being a negative status group, not solely internally generated nor can they be solely externally generated, as is evidenced by the class-differentiated priority of values.

To understand the lower class and the "culture of poverty" in a proper light requires an accounting for both the intraaction and the interaction of the poor with the non-poor, through what shall be termed a "relational" perspective, which has been derived from an extension and modification of Erving Goffman's (1963b) work on the sociology of "stigma" (also see Matza, 1966b). It should be noted that, while the term "interactional" would seem to be the more accepted term for this perspective in the vocabulary of American sociology, the term "relational" is to be preferred precisely because of the emphasis on both intra- and interaction, and because the term "interaction" is more frequently associated with "face-to-face" behavior, whereas the discussion here shall deal not with "primary" but with "secondary" relations. The next chapter will develop the argument of the stigma of poverty—that is, that poverty in the United States in particular is a stigma which produces characteristic effects, as do the types of stigma discussed by Goffman. Once established, the individual and collective reactions to and effects of the stigma will be discussed, which will then present a more clear and accurate picture of the configuration involved. At that point we shall be in a position to reflect back upon the nature of the relationship between poverty and the patterns that have been discussed as composing the cluster of traits which characterize the lower class style of life.

Chapter 4

THE STIGMA OF POVERTY

The sociological study of poverty and the poor should include, it is argued, not only the behavior of the poor themselves but also the nature of the relationship between the poor and the non-poor, specifically, the perceptions and the definitions which the non-poor have of the poor in American society. It is our contention that poverty in American society falls within the realm of "stigma," and we shall now proceed to analyze it as such. We begin with the development of stigma, and then we shall examine responses to stigma.

THE DEVELOPMENT OF STIGMA

When we meet someone for the first time, Goffman (1936b) tells us we immediately form certain impressions and evaluations of that individual, and we proceed to relate to him (or her) on the basis of expectations derived from these impressions and evaluations. This pattern is so typical that we are, in fact, unaware that we have formed these expectations until they are, for one reason or another, called into question. It is only at this point that we may become aware that we have been making certain assumptions about the individual which are actually unwarranted. We "realize" that he is not the individual we thought him to be, and the whole nature of our relationship must be shifted accordingly. It is in terms of this process that stigma becomes important:

> While the stranger is present before us, evidence can arise of his possessing an attribute that makes him different from others in the category of persons available for him to be, and of a less desirable kind—in the extreme, a person who is quite thoroughly bad, or dangerous, or weak. He is thus reduced in our minds from a whole and usual person to a tainted, discounted one. Such an attribute is a stigma. (Goffman 1963b, pp. 2-3)

It is not the attribute, per se, that is a stigma, but the "definition of the situation" or the social perception of the attribute which deems it a stigma. Stigma must be seen in terms of what Goffman calls "language of relationships"—that is, in the social context. He cites several examples, such as going to the library, which may be perfectly "normal" for a middle class boy, but which would be a stigma for a professional criminal. Or, a physical defect which someone who wanted to fight in the army might seek to conceal, whereas if that same individual wanted to get out of the army, he might go to the army hospital, where not having a physical defect might cause him to be discredited.

In his discussion of the various types of stigma, Goffman suggests three types: physical stigma-deformities, "tribal stigma of race, nation, and religion," and "blemishes of individual character perceived as weak will, domineering or unnatural passions, treacherous and rigid beliefs, and dishonesty, these being inferred from a known record of, for example, mental disorder, imprisonment, addiction, alcoholism, homosexuality, unemployment, suicidal attempts, and radical political behavior" (1963, p. 4). With all three types of stigma, the process, the effect, is the same; they interfere with what otherwise might have been a normal social relationship, because of their "undesired differentness from what we had anticipated" (p. 5).

We have stated that the objective in this chapter is to examine poverty as a stigma. Two points of clarification must be interjected at this juncture. First of all, it must be reemphasized that when reference is made to the poor and the non-poor and their respective patterns of behavior and personality developments, this does not mean that this refers to all of the poor and all of the non-poor. With the poor in particular, the evidence clearly indicates that most of the poor are not criminals, are not schizophrenics, etc.

Secondly, this analysis is not an exercise in blaming or finding a scapegoat; certainly not "victim blaming" (Ryan, 1971). It is the intent of this analysis to explore and understand, not to point a finger of blame at either the poor or the non-poor. On the contrary, the poor cannot be blamed for they are the subjects of the stigmatization, and the non-poor cannot be blamed for the stigmatization which has deep roots in this country's cultural history. In any case, "blaming" is not a positive factor in the amelioration of a problem; rather, it is a conscience-soothing method of doing nothing toward problem solving.

We would suggest that the stigma of poverty is a special type of stigma which attributes to the poor a status of being "less than human," and that the stigma has taken various shapes at different historical stages. Without positing any historical process to its development, we shall demonstrate that the stigma was initially attributed to the poor as a group stigma, that as the result of the history of government social welfare legislation and the subsequent professionalization of social work, the stigma became individualized, and that with the focusing of sociologists upon the poor in the past several decades in the United States, the stigma of poverty is once again becoming a group stigma. Thus, while the stigma of poverty cannot be pigeonholed neatly into any of Goffman's three types, it has at times resembled the "blemishes of individual character" type. Moreover, in recent years it has taken on, in addition, a strong dosage of "tribal stigma of race," because of the strong identification or association in the minds of many of welfare poor with blacks. That this association is unfounded to a great extent is irrelevant in terms of the stigma, because, as was stated previously, what is important is the "language of relationships," or what W. I. Thomas (1966) called, "the definition of the situation": "If a situation is defined as real, it is real in its consequences." There is little doubt that this situation is defined as real by many of America's non-poor, and probably by many poor as well (see United States Department of Health, Education and Welfare, 1971).

Our conception of the stigma of poverty is very similar to that of David Matza's (1966) conception of "the disreputable poor." Matza emphasizes a point which we have argued, that [t]he term disreputable introduces no personal judgment but takes account of the judgments made by other members of society; to ignore the stigma that adheres to this special kind of poverty is to miss one of its key aspects" (p. 628). We would, however, broaden the locale of the stigma and, indeed, argue that there is a ripple effect running from the central locus of the stigmatized or disreputable poor to all poor and, perhaps, even to almost the entire lower class.

It is somewhat difficult to define precisely which segment of the poor population constitutes the disreputable poor. As Matza puts it, "The search for the disreputable poor will, of necessity, yield extremely crude estimates subject to wide margins of error" (p. 628). After reviewing several conceptions, Matza concludes that

> pauperism comes closest to what is conveyed by the term, "disreputable poverty." Though there are differences, many of the features of disreputable poverty are implicit in the conception of pauperism. The concept of pauperism harbored the ideas of disaffiliation and immobilization that, taken together, indicate the outcasting from modern society suggested by Thomas and Znaniecki. Pauperism, like vice, "declasses a man definitely, puts him outside both the old and new hierarchy. Beggars, tramps, criminals, prostitutes, have no place in the class hierarchy." (p. 643)

Whereas Matza discusses four types of disreputable poor—"dregs," "newcomers," "skidders," and "the infirm" (pp. 644-654), we would argue, on the basis of evidence which will be presented in the next chapter, that these four groups form the core and those closest to that core, but that the stigma and its effects can be found with decreasing severity throughout the lower class. We shall see that in the judgment of the members of the society, one's being a recipient of certain types of assistance is seen as sufficient evidence that the individual is morally defective, not to be trusted and should be constrained in some way by society. Receipt of services of some types may be sufficient visibility to have oneself labeled, and perceived of, as being disreputably poor or, at least, stigmatized.

We should also note that the stigma of poverty is often coupled with other stigmata. For example, among the disreputable poor discussed by Matza there are newcomers; for them, there is the dual stigma of poverty and the "tribal stigma of race, nation, and religion." The black AFDC recipient would, presumably, experience the effects of these combined stigma most severely. Or, to cite another example, the infirm poor would be the subjects of the dual stigma of poverty and physical stigma-deformities.

If we imagine the stigma of poverty to be strongest at the center and inversely related to the distance from that center, then the stigma of poverty may be diagramatically presented in the following manner:

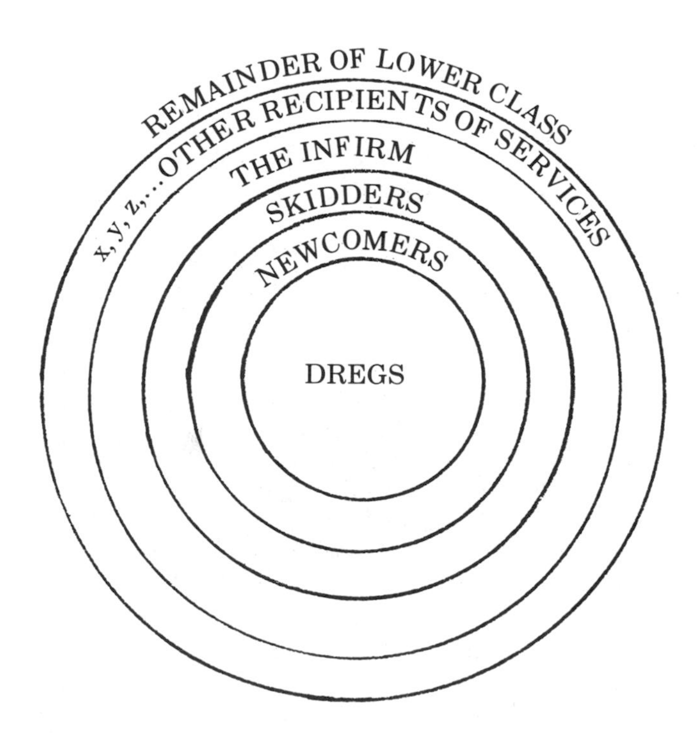

Fig. 4.1 *The stigma of poverty as it applies to various types of poor.*

The extent to which the poor are thought of as having weak character and being responsible for their own condition is conspicuous in a nationwide study of American political beliefs conducted n 1964 by the Gallup and Harris organizations for Lloyd A. Free and Hadley Cantril (1968). This study revealed that in 1964, a year in which idealism concerning the elimination or eradication of poverty was very high, the majority of Americans saw "lack of effort" as the major source of poverty. When the responses were broken down by income, the following were the results:

Table 4.1 *Causes of poverty by family income*

	Under $5,000	$5,000-$9,999	$10,000 and over
Circumstances	28%	23%	23%
Lack of effort	25	38	44
Both	43	36	32
Don't know	4	3	1
	100%	100%	100%

Source: Lloyd A. Free and Hadley Cantril. *The Political Beliefs of Americans: A Study of Public Opinion*. Copyright © 1967 by Rutgers, The State University. Reprinted by permission of the Rutgers University Press.

Note that even in the "Under $5,000" category, those who are themselves in or very near the poverty population, the majority saw "lack of effort," either alone or combined with "circumstances," as the root of the problem.

In a study dealing specifically with attitudes toward welfare, David Kallen and Dorothy Miller (1971) found 81% of the whites and 78% of the blacks interviewed agreeing with the statement: "There are too many people receiving welfare who should be working" (p. 88). Similarly, Joe Feagin (1975) reports that in his nationwide study, 84% of the sample agreed with the same statement (p. 104). We shall examine the validity of this statement at a later point. For the present, the large number of those agreeing with it indicates an essentially negative attitude toward welfare and, by implication, toward the poor.

To grasp the full implications of this attitude, we must now direct our attention to the history of governmental involvement with the poor, specifically, from the first Poor Laws in England through contemporary American social welfare policies, which covers a span of approximately 600 years (de Schweinitz, 1961). We begin with the English Poor Laws because, as we mentioned, they mark the beginning of government social welfare in the West and because of their significant impact upon subsequent social welfare legislation and policies in the United States (cf, Piven

& Cloward, 1971; Woodroofe, 1966). We find that throughout this period, in both England and later in the United States, poverty has been considered a negative condition, that the poor have been perceived of as "not quite human," and that social welfare legislation has been primarily concerned with the maintenance of public order (the order of the non-poor), rather than with the condition and care of the poor on their own account.

Furthermore, we shall see how the legitimations and rationalizations for this perception and approach to the poor have undergone changes with the changes in the general prevailing *Weltanschauungen*, from the early moralistic to the 18th and 19th century naturalistic to the 20th century scientific views. The effect of all of these labels is to stereotype the poor, to isolate and distort their position by concealing their roles in terms of their interaction with both themselves and the non-poor. These legitimations and rationalizations serve as what Goffman (1963) calls "stigma-theories," or ideologies which "explain his (the stigmatized's) inferiority and account for the danger which it represents," and thus justify our "exercise [of] varieties of discriminations, through which effectively, if not unthinkingly, [we] reduce his life chances" (p. 5).

Governmental concern with the problem of poverty in England may be said to have emerged in the 14th century. Prior to that time, poverty was the concern of the Church. Within the Church, dramatic redefinitions were taking place. In the early Church, the poor, as a group, were deemed to be of the highest moral status, and the rich were demoted to second-class spiritual status. However, as the result of internal struggles within the Church, there had developed by the 14th century a hierarchy of types of poverty and a hostile attitude toward begging and pauperism (Walter, 1970, pp. 45-67). The first two stages in the development of the stigma of poverty were, thus, the casting of a collective status upon the poor, albeit an initially high status, and then the transformation of many of these into a negative status group.

When the government intervened in the mid-14th century, it did so not so much out of concern for the condition of the poor on their own account, but rather out of a concern for the dominant non-poor. The immediate cause of concern was the result of the growing problem of maintaining security.

> The king and his nobles were intent upon an altogether different object, namely, maintaining order—that is (as governments always understand it) the maintenance of the then-existing order, based on a social hierarchy of rulers and ruled, of landowners and those who belonged to the land. (Webb & Webb, 1963, p. 23)

Insofar as the specific causes for the concern with maintaining public order at that particular time, de Schweinitz (1961) traces it to the decline of feudalism:

> By the middle of the fourteenth century feudalism was nearing its end. Wages had come largely into use. They were both a symbol and a means of the emancipation of the laborer from serfdom. The number of men who worked for anyone who would pay them, and where they pleased, had steadily grown. Along with this advance toward freedom, however, went the loss of economic security that inhered in having a master. Now, when misfortune came, there was no patron in whom the liberated individual had a guarantee of help. Lacking this, many persons when in need turned to mendicancy or theft. To the landowners, the new conditions were a source of great dissatisfaction. They were losing much of their control over labor. In addition, there was a menace to safety and property of men who existed on the basis of what they could take by stealth or force. (p. 3)

The Webbs (1963) find three major causes for concern with maintaining public order at the time. In addition to the rise of mendicancy and theft, which resulted from the decline of feudalism, there was the Black Death and the general economic upheaval, which resulted from both the Black Death and the decline of feudalism:

> One main object of the Legislature in these Acts was doubtless the prevention of the disorder, violence and other crime to which an extensive vagrancy gave rise. We cannot, however, overlook the fact that, from the fourteenth century onwards, and especially after the Black Death (1349)—itself only one of a score of pestilences in that century—the statutes show a further intention. The feudal organisation of the manor, with its basis in serfdom and customary occupancy of land upon obligations of personal service, was breaking down. A new class of freedmen, becoming free labourers, was thus emerging...The shock which the Great Pestilence itself, and the resulting scarcity and high wages of labour, gave to the economic organisation of the English village and the ecclesiastical parish was perhaps unparalleled in severity. (Webb & Webb, 1963, p. 24)

This concern with poverty as deriving from a concern with the maintenance of public order was not limited to the 14th century; the continuing interest and concern of the government in England with poverty remained primarily a direct result of the government's concern with public security into the 16th century:

> It may be safely said that the steady concern of the Tudors with the problem of poverty flowed from the almost obsessive preoccupation of these great rulers with the question of public order. Henry VII, his son, and his granddaughter all shared an intuitive sensitivity in this matter and were quick to lash out when the slightest threat to public security appeared in any part of the realm. This concern was surely part of their jealous conception of the meaning of sovereignty and their abiding resolution to secure the realm and their throne from the chronic disorder of the preceding century. We may well believe that these monarchs were not moved by sentiments of piety or of pity as they resolutely addressed themselves to the problem of poverty, but they were at the same time deeply persuaded that unrelieved and uncontrolled poverty was the most fertile breeding ground for local disorders which might be a kind of social contagion flame across the whole realm. Hence it was that the immense power of the Crown was steadily addressed to the problem of poverty. (Jordan, 1959, p. 77)[13]

The change in attitude toward poverty during the 14th century, which, fully developed by the 16th century, saw "that hungry men were simply invincibly idle men, that poverty was a consequence of moral fault" (Jordan, 1959, p. 80) resulted in adoption of repressive policies to deal with the poor. The perception of the poor as being morally defective is the dominant theme of the stigma of poverty and is implicitly rooted in the broader conservative view of the nature of man as intrinsically evil. As Lenski (1966) summarizes it: "Historically, conservatives have been distrustful of man's basic nature and have emphasized the need for restraining institutions" (p. 22). The implementation of repressive policies toward the poor is a manifestation of one of these restraining social institutions. Both in this chapter and the next we shall see that the persistent call for repressive policies to deal with the poor is often legitimized by their alleged inherent moral defectiveness, and by the belief that they will only cease to be morally defective when they are "purified" through the process of forced rigid resocialization which is the objective of the harsh repression.

The earliest among these repressive policies were the Statutes of Laborers of 1349, which forbade the giving of alms to "valient beggars"

---

[13] We might note, in passing, that much of the governmental concern with the problem of poverty in mid-20th century America grew, also, out of a concern with maintaining public order, as a direct consequence of the perceived growth of the problem of crime and delinquency—the entire theoretical framework for the Community Action Program (CAP) has its roots and subsequent development in juvenile delinquency theories and projects (cf. Donovan, 1967, especially Chapter 3, pp. 39-48; Morris & Rein, 1967, especially Chapters 1 and 2; Moynihan, 1969, pp. 170-177; Piven & Cloward, 1971; Rubin, 1967, pp. 5-18, a revised version appears in *The Annals*, Vol. 385, Sept. 1969, pp. 14-29).

who "refuse to labor, giving themselves to theft and other abominations" (de Schweinitz, 1961, p. 1). Later amendments to this law, in 1351 and 1388, restricted the geographic mobility of servants and laborers. The amendments of 1388, however, for the first time recognized the possibility of unemployment as being related to the labor supply (pp. 7-8).

Much of the legislation well into the 16th century dealt with repressive policies toward vagrance. In 1531, the government under Henry VIII for the first time recognized governmental responsibility for the care of the poor, established what may be the first "means test" for determining eligibility for the right to beg, and provided areas within which begging was permitted (de Schweinitz, 1961, pp. 20-21). Vagrants were whipped and unlicensed poor were heavily fined (Jordan, 1959). The Act of 1536 attempted to ease the plight of the impotent poor, but persisted with "the stubbornly held persuasion that there were no genuinely unemployed poor and that vagrancy could be driven from the realm by the application of the criminal law" (Jordan, 1959, p. 85). This Act required local parishes to care for their poor and to establish a method for collecting and administering donations for that care by local officials. Subsequently, by 1563, these donations, formerly voluntary, became compulsory (de Schweinitz, 1961, p. 25). The first clear distinction between vagrants and impotent poor (later to be known, respectively, as undeserving and deserving poor) was in the early Elizabethean statutes, specifically 14 Elizabeth, Chapter 5, in 1572. This was the beginning of a process which stretched over several hundred years in which there was a decomposition and trend toward individualization of the stigma of poverty. In this Act vagrants were defined as "all able-bodied men without land or master who could not explain the source of their livelihood, all such men who declined to accept employment, and by prescription certain classes of men, such as peddlars, tinkers, minstrels, who all too often had proved to be vagrants" (de Schweinitz, 1966, p. 88). In addition, this Act is of special significance in that it "marks the beginning in England of the legislation of taxes for relief" (p. 26). Thirdly, this Act gave the overseer of the poor the responsibility "of putting rogues and vagabonds to work" (p. 25).

Several additional acts were subsequently passed, the most significant being 39 Elizabeth (1597), which spelled out the responsibilities of the community for its poor, confirmed the almshouse as part of the relief program, and established the mutual responsibility of parents and children for each other's support (de Schweinitz, 1961, p. 27). Perhaps the major impetus for the passage of this Act was the severe economic depression in England which began with the heavy rains in 1594 and resulted in poor harvests for the next five years. The worst year was 1596, with high unemployment, high prices, and a critical threat of famine. The country was in a state of panic, riots broke out, and capital punishment was meted out to felons. This experience forced the recognition that unemployment was not necessarily an indication of idleness, irresponsibility, or immorality, and in October of 1597 Parliament convened with a complete consideration and debate on poverty and relief. The condition, debate, and legislation led to the first major legal categorization of types of poor (Jordan, 1959, pp. 92ff).

The next major amendment to the Poor Laws came in 1662 with the passage of the Law of Settlement, "an amendment that has influenced the administration of relief down to the present time," and which "represented the most extreme and cruel form of localism that England had known previously or has known since" (de Schweinitz, 1961, p. 39). This law empowered the local authorities to return any individual who *might someday* apply for relief to his former residence.

> This statute was a throwback to the days of serfdom and to the theory that the worker belonged where he was born. It represented both a culmination of the post-feudal effort to imprison the laborer in his parish and the most extreme development of parochialism which recognized no human need that could possibly be charged to its neighbor. (p. 40)

Despite the criticism of the law by many, including Adam Smith, who, in his *The Wealth of Nations* (1937) said of it, "There is scarce a poor man in England of forty years of age, I will venture to say, who has not in some part of his life felt himself cruelly oppressed by this ill-contrived law of settlements" (Book I, Chapter 8, Part II, p. 141), it was not until 1795 that the law was amended to allow the removal and return of an individual only after he actually applied for relief (de Schweinitz, 1961, p. 44).

Lest anyone be amazed that principles of local exclusion could persist for so long, bear in mind that it was not until 1969 that the United States Supreme Court struck down the state residency requirements for obtaining welfare in the United States (*Shapiro v. Thompson,* 394 U.S. 618, 1969) and even after that ruling, a number of states (New York and Connecticut in particular) attempted, ultimately unsuccessfully, to reinstitute residency requirements.

At about the same time as the passage of the Law of Settlement, a new idea which was aimed at tackling the problem of poverty and, simultaneously, helping industry to expand began to gain in popularity. This approach was initiated by the Quakers to establish "Colleges of Industry" where the poor could pool their efforts for their own good (de Schweinitz, 1961, pp. 48 ff; Polanyi, 1957, p. 105). The idea never reached the full blossom its advocates had hoped for, but despite the strong opposition of

Daniel Defoe (who wrote *Giving Alms No Charity, and Employing the Poor a Grievance to the Nation*, in 1704) and others, it was popular, only to later result in disappointment as an unfulfilled promise.

The employment of the unemployed having failed, the period 1722-1782 witnessed the implementation of a system of workhouses where men, women, and children who received relief were forced to eat, sleep, and work. The rules in the workhouses were very rigid, and violation resulted in punishments which "included the stocks, the dungeon, denial of meals, refusal of permission to leave the house" (de Schweinitz, 1961, p. 62).

The 18th century gave birth to two important schools of political and economic philosophy, both of which were to have profound influence on Poor Law legislation and attitudes toward poverty and the poor for years to come. The first of these had its origins in the writings of Adam Smith, the "father of modern economics" and the doctrine of "laissez-faire." The second, which reached its full maturity in the following century in the form of Social Darwinism, had its seeds planted by one Joseph Townsend, who in 1786 published a small book entitled, *A Dissertation on the Poor Laws: By a Well-Wisher to Mankind*, and which "never ceased to occupy men's minds for another century and a half."[14] His position is based on what allegedly occurred on the island of Juan Fernandez, where that Spanish admiral (mid-16th century) had placed a number of goats, which "could readily obey the first commandment, to increase and multiply," and which provided food for the English privateers who were pirating Spanish ships. In order to cut off their enemy's food supply, the Spaniards introduced to the island a greyhound dog and a bitch, which themselves multiplied and greatly reduced the number of goats.

> Had they [the goats] been totally destroyed, the dogs likewise must have perished. But as many of the goats retired to the craggy rocks, where the dogs could never follow them, descending only for short intervals to feed with fear and circumspection in the vallies, few of these, besides the careless and the rash, became a prey; and none but the most watchful, strong, and active of the dogs could get a sufficiency of food. Thus a new kind of balance was established. The weakest of both species were among the first to pay the debt of nature; the most active and vigorous preserved their lives. (Townsend, 1971, p. 38).

[14]Polanyi (1957, p. 111) cites him as "William Townsend"; de Schweinitz (1961, pp. 115-116) cites him as "Joseph Townsend, a clergy man"; Robert L. Heilbroner (1967, p. 80) cites him as "a Reverend James 'Townshend"; the book has subsequently been reprinted (1971) with a Foreword by Ashley Montague and an Afterword by Mark Neuman, and the author's name is, in fact, Joseph Townsend. All references which follow are to this 1971 edition.

From this story, Townsend derives his conclusion, which in the next century came to be known as the Social Darwinist principle of natural selection:

> It is the quantity of food which regulates the numbers of the human species. In the woods, and in the *savage state*, there can be few inhabitants, but of these there will only be a proportionable few to suffer want. As long as food is plenty they will continue to increase and multiply; and every man will have ability to support his family, or to relieve his friends, in proportion to his activity and strength. The weak must depend upon the precarious bounty of the strong; and, sooner or later, the lazy will be left to suffer the natural consequence of their indolence. Should they introduce a community of goods, and at the same time leave every man at liberty to marry, they would at first increase their numbers, but not the sum total of their happiness, till by degrees, all being equally reduced to want and misery, the weakly would be the first to perish. (p. 38)

And it is because of this principle that the Poor Laws "are not only unjust, oppressive, and impolitic...; but they proceed upon principles which border on absurdity, as professing to accomplish that which, in the very nature and constitution of the world, is impracticable" (p. 36). They are impracticable because it is in the very nature of society that there will be some who must suffer want; yet the laws are based on the premise "that in England no man, even though by his indolence, improvidence, prodigality, and vice, he may have brought himself to poverty, shall ever suffer want." But since some must suffer want, the only question can be, "Who is most worthy to suffer cold and hunger, the prodigal or the provident, the slothful or the diligent, the virtuous or the vicious"? (p. 36).

While Townsend's tract did not have immediate effect—in fact, the Speenhamland Law of 1795 instituted reforms in the exact opposite direction—it did have a profound effect on Malthus, directly, and Darwin, indirectly, and on the Poor Law reforms of 1834. The fallacy or at least misleading character of his argument, the fact that it implies that *all* the poor are indolent, improvident, prodigal, and vice addicts, in no way detracted from its effect, neither during the 19th nor the 20th century.

The Speenhamland Law, or Act of 1795, was actually not a part of the Poor Laws; rather, it was a labor law, but it did have a definite impact on the Poor Laws. The Law came upon the recommendations of the justices of Berkshire who met in Speenhamland in May of 1795 and legally established the "right to live" that is, it guaranteed each person a minimum income, so that if his earnings fell below the minimum, he would receive an income supplement from relief. While the Law was intended to ease the plight of laborers and the poor, it actually had the opposite effect, because the public funds resulted in the restoration of civil order through the enforcement of work at very low wages, and, most importantly, the Law resulted in the "destruction of the work incentive" on the part of those who were working at a very low scale (which was not uncommon, since the employer could get workers at almost any pay), because these laborers soon realized that they could get their minimum income no matter what the quality or quantity of their work.[15] In any case, "[i]n the long run the result was ghastly" (Polanyi, 1957, p. 80). And the trend toward liberalization came to an end with the Poor Law reforms of 1834.

In the meantime, in 1798, Thomas Robert Malthus published his famous *Essay on Population*, where he forecasted the inevitability of famine as the result of the geometric population increase and arithmetic food supply increase. By maintaining the poor on relief, he said, the food supply is spread thinner, raising its cost and ultimately subjecting the non-poor to impoverishment.

The growing body of thought represented by Townsend and Malthus, the backfiring of the Speenhamland Law, and finally the outbreak of riots by the poor in 1830, led to the reform of the Poor Laws in 1834. Accordingly, the Report of the Royal Commission for Inquiring into the Administrative and Practical Operation of the Poor Laws "inaugurated the doctrine of *less eligibility*, the theory that throughout the nineteenth century and into the twentieth controlled the approach of English government to the relief of destitution" (de Schweinitz, 1961, p. 124, emphasis in original). The doctrine of less eligibility meant that persons on relief should be kept in a condition necessarily worse than that of the lowest paid worker not on relief, the objective being to make relief undesirable and to provide the recipient with a clear and strong incentive to get off the relief rolls. To this end, the Act of 1834 created a central body of Poor Law Commissioners which organized and oversaw all of the local Boards of Guardians, ordered each local Board to build a workhouse, and ruled that no person would receive relief unless he agreed to enter the workhouse, where the "deserving poor" could be separated from the lazy and indolent. The workhouse was, in effect, a prison (although anyone could leave if he so wished), in that all "inmates" of the workhouse lost their rights of citizenship (if they had previously had them), were required to wear distinctive workhouse clothing, were required to do menial tasks, and were separated from their families (the whole nuclear family was required to

[15] We should point out that it is the fear of the recurrence of precisely this type of a situation which is one of the arguments employed to prevent the instituting of any system of guaranteed annual income in the United States, despite its advocacy from many sectors of the population in recent years; see Family Assistance Program discussion, in Chapter 5.

enter the workhouse, but men, women, and children were all separated from each other; only infants younger than three years were allowed to be with their mothers).

The Poor Law of 1834 was, in essence, a palatable enactment of the Malthusian principle; it attempted to force the "pauper" to extricate himself from his own moral depravity. As Malthus maintained, the only cure to social ills was moral restraint. But it was not an uncompromising Malthusian law, because that would have meant no law at all and no charity of any kind, even private, except in the most extreme cases (Poynter, 1969, pp. 156-158).[16]

In an attempt to classify the poor more adequately, the law established four types: "the aged and really impotent; the children; the able-bodied females; the able-bodied males." This classification was a further indication of differentiation and individualization of the stigma of poverty. The basic stigma was, as indicated earlier, poverty as a manifestation of moral defect. The classification of the poor indicated that there were perceived to be gradations or levels of moral defect among the poor,with the core (or most defective) being male paupers. In general, however, poverty was seen as due to the moral failure of the individual. "The report placed the burden of destitution upon the shoulders of the individual. Poverty was regarded as essentially an indication of moral fault in the person requiring relief. He was held very little short of exclusively responsible for his condition" (de Schweinitz, 1961, p. 126).

The reforms of 1834, in any case, proved to be unsuccessful, and the mid-19th century witnessed a growing dissatisfaction and debate over the poor laws, with criticism coming from both the laissez-faire and Social Darwinist camps on one side, and collectivist Utilitarians (e.g., J. S. Mill) on the other (see Polanyi, 1957, especially Chapter 10). By mid-century, a proliferation of private charity organizations had sprung up ubiquitously; as is usually the case, they were largely uncoordinated and often competitive. Thus, in 1870, the Society for Organising Charitable Relief and Repressing Mendicity met for the first time, with the expressed goal of coordinating the efforts and formulating guidelines for London's many charitable organizations. The Society believed that indiscriminate charity was demoralizing and self-defeating in that it increased dependence and was the cause of much poverty. The aim of charity should be to "encourage independence, strengthen character, and help to preserve the

---

[16] Poynter maintains that the Law had the definite mark of J. Bentham's Pauper Plan of the mid-18th century in its "middle way between prodigality and starvation" (p. 320), and he concludes that the "general principles on which it [Bentham's] was based bear so many resemblances to the principles of 1834 that the onus of proof is surely on those who would deny Bentham's influence on the Act which created the new Poor Law" (p. 327).

family as the fundamental unit of society" (Woodroofe, 1966, p. 28). The source of poverty, thus, was dependence, weak character, and the disintegration of the family unit. In the view of Charles Steward Loch, who was appointed Secretary to the Society in 1875, the fault with those who failed to achieve independence was their own, not society's. Those who were beyond help from private charities, either because they were immoral or because they suffered from chronic poverty, were the only ones to be handled by the State under the Poor Laws. "Poor relief is for those who, for some reason or other, are defaulters in the contract of social obligation. They do not maintain themselves. They throw the fulfillment of their obligations on others—on the State, on members of the community," and therefore deserved the harsh and niggardly treatment under the Poor Laws (Woodroofe, 1966, p. 35). The major problem with the Poor Laws, according to Loch, was that under them and under the unorganized system of charity which then existed, charity was not dispensed to meet the individual needs of the recipient, but was rather "doled out on such terms as are often required by the trust deeds of old foundations: so much apiece to so many old women on a fixed day of the year, or so much as dowry on their marriage to spinsters of a certain age and good character resident in a certain place" (Loch, 1892, p. 34). Loch summed up his conclusions on the distribution of relief in four points: First, relief is to be given only in the most dire of circumstances, and should never be given to the extent that the recipient will come to rely on others to fulfill his own obligations. Secondly, "When a request for relief of this kind is made, the question asked should be, 'Ought I not refuse?' rather than, 'Ought I not give'?[17] And then, 'If I ought to give, how can I prevent in the future the recurrence of distress due to this cause?' " (Loch, 1892, p. 35). Third, where "vice is the cause of distress...plainly relief by itself serves no good purpose. The evil itself must be given up, and to that end persuasion and reform with, sometimes, medical aid will be alone of service." (p. 36). Finally, while there must be provision for relief for those who are "incorrigible," it must always be dispensed "in a manner that will not attract applicants" and should be kept within the closest limits, or they will, almost certainly, create a demand for such relief as they afford. To be idle, even under the most uncomfortable conditions, is sweeter to some than to labour" (p. 36).

The society operated under the assumption that there were deserving and undeserving poor, and though it couldn't arrive at any steadfast formula for distinguishing between the two categories and finally left it at

[17] Along these same lines, Richard M. Titmuss (1968) has summarized the functions of means tests today. "The aim may be to deter people from using or 'abusing' a service; to induce a sense of inferiority among those using a public service..." (p. 116).

"not likely to benefit" in place of "undeserving," the Charity Organisation Society (COS) stressed the value of treating each case separately and keeping a record and raising funds for each case individually. It is from these beginnings that the casework approach to social work, with its stress on the interview, home visit, investigation, etc. evolved. In terms of the historical development of the stigma of poverty, Loch and the subsequent social work profession must be credited with dramatically transforming the stigma of poverty from its heretofore collective character to a much more individual character. By emphasizing the need to treat each case individually, the stigma of poverty resembled a tribal stigma less and less and became much more a stigma of individual character. Once it became a stigma of individual character, it may have opened up alternatives for the individual's adjustment to the stigma. This point will be elaborated upon when we discuss adjustments to stigma in contemporary America.

Alongside the developing professionalization of social work, the process of rationalization and bureaucratization analyzed by Max Weber set in, and the introduction of "expertise" and "technical knowledge" had the latent function of further individualizing the stigma of poverty. The transition of the stigma of poverty from a tribal-like stigma or group stigma to a more individualistic one was accelerated by the technocratization of that group which saw itself (and was seen) as the experts on poverty and the poor.

The COS saw its function not merely as a voluntary charitable organization, but, more importantly, as a means for bringing about a better society where each man helped his neighbor; misfortune was to be erased through the combined resources spurred on by the COS. It was, to a great extent, based on the *individualistic* doctrine of self-help espoused by Herbert Spencer (1961), who condemned the *(collectivist)* Poor Laws in the almost identical terms as did Townsend and Malthus in the preceding century—namely, that they contribute to the biological and moral decay of the society:

> If men who, for a score of generations, had by preference bred from their worst-tempered horses and their least-sagacious dogs, were then to wonder because their horses were vicious and their dogs stupid, we should think the absurdity of their policy paralleled only by the absurdity of their astonishment; but human beings instead of inferior animals being in question, no absurdity is seen either in the policy or in the astonishment. (p. 337)

Needless to say, while the COS assumed the Spencerian view of the Poor Laws and was essentially anti-collectivist in the sense of the state assuming the responsibility for and intervening in social welfare, it did see each individual *qua* individual, having a responsibility for his neighbor.

From the outset, social work attempted to intervene in the isolation and ignorance between the poor and the non-poor as to "how the other half lives." In 1877, Octavia Hill, a pioneer in the training of social workers, admonished those involved in assistance not to think of the poor as a separate species: "Depend upon it, if we thought of the poor primarily as husbands, wives, sons, and daughters, members of households, as we are ourselves, instead of contemplating them as a different class, we should recognize better how the house training and high ideals of home duty was our best preparation for work among them" (quoted in Woodroofe, 1966, p. 49). In addition, Miss Hill and other early social workers were struck with the moral degradation that seemed so often to accompany poverty. Describing her childhood neighborhood in London, she wrote, "There the first knowledge of misery and poverty came to me, the first real feeling of poverty for ourselves. There...I sat and watched, through the great windows, the London poor pass in rain and fog. There I sat and cried...at the rememberance of Tottenham Court Road on Saturday night with its haggard faces" (quoted in Woodroofe, 1966, p. 50). As a result of these "realizations," social work aimed at uplifting the poor from their degradation, overcoming the dependence and apathy of the poor, and imbuing the non-poor with a sense of responsibility toward the poor.

It is important to understand, however, that while Octavia Hill recognized the isolation of the poor from the non-poor and attempted to bring the two together so that they might recognize each other as human beings, this does not mean that she saw no stigma in poverty. Quite the contrary. and she too adhered to the belief that the poor themselves were responsible for their poverty:

> I believe our irregular alms to the occupant of the miserable room, to the shoeless flower-seller, are tending to keep a whole class on the very brink of pauperism who might be taught self-control and foresight if we would let them learn it...
>
> The street-sellers and low class desultory workers usually remain what they are by choice; a little self-control would raise them into the ranks of those who are really wanted, and who have made their way from the brink of pauperism to a securer place, and one where they are better influences. Above all is this true of the children.
>
> A little self-control would enable the daughters of most of these people to rise into the class of domestic servants; and their sons, instead of remaining street-sellers, would soon learn a trade or go to sea if they cared to do regular work. We are largely helping by our foolish gifts, to keep them herded together in crowded, dirty, badly-built rooms, among scenes of pauperism, crime, and vice. (quoted in de Schweinitz, 1961, p. 146)

Octavia Hill moved beyond the perception of poverty in terms of its being a tribal or biological stigma and had "progressed" with the changing social philosophies of her day to the point where she saw poverty as a stigma of individual character. The distinction is all-important, because the latter type of stigma is somewhat more congenial to reform than the former.

By the turn of the 20th century, while it has moved from the narrow confines of charity to a whole set of principles and techniques accompanying a social philosophy, social casework still retained many of the individualistic principles from which it was born—that is, "a set of assumptions about the nature of human society and its organization which belonged to the nineteenth century rather than the twentieth" (Woodroofe, 1966, p. 55).

While the majority in the COS saw the source of poverty as lying within the individual, others both within and without the Society, coming under the influence of the growing bodies of thought which emphasized the influence of the society and culture upon the individual, began to see the source of poverty as lying within the environment of the poor. The shift was from the individual to the social system. For example, in 1893, Miss H. Dendy of the COS proclaimed that, "Human beings cannot be treated as simple units... The man with his character such as his temperament and surroundings have made it, can only act within the limits of the community of which he is a fraction" (Quoted in Woodroofe, 1966, p. 60). This new awareness of the community as a contributory factor to the individual's poverty, and the resulting cognizance of the need to mobilize the community resources to meet the needs of the individual, led to the development of the group work and community organization approach to social work (Woodroofe, 1966, pp. 60-74).

The effects of this change in perception, for our purposes, is twofold. Firstly, by redirecting attention as to the source of the problem from the individual to the social system, there is a softening of the stigma of poverty, for the crux of the stigma is that it defines the source of the problem within the poor, either as a group or individually, and attributes responsibility to the poor. The shift in focus from the individual to the social system means, *ipso facto*, that the individual is not responsible *in toto* for his condition which is therefore not attributable to *his* moral depravity.

Moreover, the group work and community organization approaches attempt to integrate individual poor within communities of similarly stigmatized individuals and may facilitate their developing collective reactions to stigma. The extent to which this is feasible would depend, in part, on whether they can come to perceive themselves as real community capable of collective reaction. This point will be discussed in more detail when we deal with reactions to stigma.

On the other hand, it should also be pointed out that these new approaches to social work can redound in a reassertion of the stigma of poverty as a group stigma, precisely because they focus upon the poor as a group. Again, this would depend to an extent upon the group's ability to develop collective reactions to stigma.

In 19th century America, these attitudes and approaches to poverty were transplanted.[18] These were adapted to the prevailing ideologies which, on the one hand, from a religious perspective saw poverty as "a fortunate necessity which led the poor into paths of industry and the rich into acts of charity" (Woodroofe, 1966, p. 82), and on the other hand, saw poverty as a misfortune, unnecessary in the land of golden opportunity. No one who was willing to work need remain poor. Where it existed, poverty was seen as "punishment meted out to the poor for their indolence, inefficiency or improvidence; or else it was interpreted in terms of heredity, intoxicating drink, 'degeneration,' partisan politics, or, as in one case, the unrestricted liberty allowed to vagrant and degraded women" (p. 83). Note how these fit almost identically with the two types of stigma which have been discussed. In such an atmosphere, the casework approach was, of course, the only one feasible.

It was not until the early part of the 20th century in America that the attitude toward poverty began to shift from the individual, with society being seen as the source, and this shift came about as the result of a shift in focus from pauperism to poverty. Here we can see the softening of the stigma of poverty which results from the redirection of the source of the problem, which we just discussed. In 1906, the economist and social worker, Edward T. Devine, proclaimed that behind alcoholism, sweatshops, and child labor lay that group which profits from exploitation, and he called on the social worker to "seek out and to strike effectively at those organized forces of evil, at those particular causes of dependency and

[18] Individual states had set up agencies to deal with social welfare in the latter part of the 19th century, and the attitude implicit in the operation of these agencies was much the same as it had been in England under the Poor Laws (cf. de Schweinitz. 1961; Piven & Cloward, 1971. especially Chapter 1, pp. 3-41; Woodroofe, 1966, Chapter 4, pp. 77-100). The principle of "less eligibility" together with many of the other policies which had as their basis the stigma of poverty under the Poor Laws in England, are found with equal vigor in the relief systems of many of the United States:

> Transferred from the Poor Laws of England to this land of abundance, the ideology of scarcity persisted till well into the twentieth century. It set great store on public penny-pinching; it assumed that human nature was bad; it took for granted the necessity for a means test to prove destitution, and claimed that, even if a recipient of relief paid the price in humiliation and loss of civil rights, the help granted him must be minimal, local and deterrent. (Woodroofe, 1966, p. 87)

intolerable conditions which are beyond the control of the individual whom they injure and whom they often destroy" (quoted in Woodroofe, 1966, p. 95). It was during those years that there was growing popular support for social controls in the economic sphere; as a result, social work moved beyond the individual casework approach to attempting to correct many of the social ills which plagued the system. Social work expanded its range of interest and influence into the areas of probation, medical social work, family social welfare, care of the handicapped, etc., and many charity—now social work—societies took on the responsibility of training their own social workers. In the United States, as in England, social work came to be regarded initially by its practitioners, "as a profession in much the same way as other men regarded law, medicine and theology" (Woodroofe, 1966, p. 97).

Social work as a profession began to come of age through the efforts of Mary Richmond and her most important book, *Social Diagnosis*, published in 1917. This was the first work which sought to conceptualize and systematically organize social work principles and practice based on the sociological knowledge of that time. Richmond organized the casework approach according to the following components; investigation, diagnosis, cooperation with all possible sources of assistance, and treatment. Each case was to be analyzed in terms of those procedures in order to understand why an individual remained dependent in spite of assistance. It is not necessary for us to elaborate on these principles and procedures; the book's importance for our purposes is twofold. First of all, the very idea of setting down principles and procedures of social work was a mark of the professionalization of the field. Secondly, the fact that it was rejected at the time of its appearance is significant. According to Woodroofe and Charlotte Towle, among others, it was rejected because it was based solely on sociological, rather than psychological and psychiatric foundations. Social work reacted against this approach and, in opposition, adopted a completely psychiatric basis for casework (Woodroofe, 1966, pp. 101-117).

With the growing influence of psychology and psychiatry during the teens of the 20th century, casework was caught in "the psychiatric deluge," and for the next two decades "clients" were seen as experiencing "inner problems, tensions and fears," "character disturbance," "emotional immaturity," and the caseworker adopted such psychoanalytic techniques as "free association," "dynamic passivity," and "therapy" as part of the "helping process," by means of which the client would begin to recognize and face his "deepseated conflicts within his personality," and thus become "emotionally rehabilitated." Together with the political and social climate of individualism in America during the 1920s, the psychiatric approach to casework gave further substance to the stigma theory which perceived poverty as a "blemish of individual character," because it gave "scientific" validation to the perception of poverty as being totally rooted in the individual, to the exclusion of any possibility of environmental influences. (cf. Woodroofe, 1966, pp. 118-147).

The Great Depression of the 1930s and the resulting New Deal had profound effects both on the involvement of government in social welfare and the attitude of and toward the profession of social work. Until that time, despite the fact that the federal government in the United States had grown in stature and in power, and the country was already one of the world's major industrial powers, social welfare was left primarily to state and local governments and volunteer agencies. Then, with the Depression and its massive unemployment, on May 12, 1933, President Franklin D. Roosevelt had the Federal Emergency Relief Act passed, and the federal government took over the administration of relief from state and local governments, under the Federal Emergency Relief Administration (FERA). Despite the possibilities of a liberal interpretation of the Act, Harry L. Hopkins, a social worker by training, who was appointed Federal Administrator of FERA made his position clear to the National Conference of Social Workers in 1933: "I am not going to hide behind the cloak of intent of Congress as to what federal funds can be used for...It is my belief that the people who fought for this bill...were trying to get it for relief of the unemployed, and not for a number of other perfectly fine and worthy objectives" (quoted in Woodroofe, 1966, pp. 164-165). "Employables" were to be sent to work, public works if need be; relief was reserved for the "unemployables." As President Roosevelt later explained to Congress, "To dole out relief in this way is to administer a narcotic, a destroyer of the human spirit. It is inimical to sound policy. It is in violation of the traditions of America. Work must be found for able-bodied destitute workers" (quoted in Woodroofe, 1966, p. 165). In 1969, President Richard M. Nixon was to echo Roosevelt, proclaiming, "what America needs now is not more welfare but more 'workfare.' " (*New York Times* 1969).

Through FERA the government brought social workers into every area of the country for the purposes of interviewing, determining eligibility, and giving assistance to the multitude which poured into FERA's social service divisions. As a result of its increased importance and demand (wrought by society's "recognition" of its value), social work began to lean more and more to the position of those who called for a planned economy. Public relief was beginning to be recognized as a public, governmental responsibility rather than a private or volunteer one, and this new recognition effected dramatic changes in the philosophy and techniques of social work. Social work adopted a new democratic philosophy which entailed the right of each individual not only to life and liberty but also "the right to make a comfortable living" (Pres. Roosevelt, quoted in Woodroofe, 1966, p. 167), and a right to receive sufficient assistance necessitated by the Depression, regardless of race, color, creed, or political persuasion, and without being demoralized and degraded as a result. The responsibility of the government was seen to involve more than just relief, and in 1935 the Social Security Act was passed, with the government now guaranteeing social insurance and other remedial and preventive services such as public assistance, maternal and child welfare services, aid to dependent children and the handicapped, and the strengthening of public health work. A new militant group of social workers now publicly proclaimed the role of social work to be not the conservative supporter of governmental policy but rather the radical social reformer. Even the less militant social workers began to call for their profession's concentration on bringing about "profound and permanent changes in our economic and social structure" (K. Lenroot, quoted in Woodroofe, 1966, p. 172). This should have resulted in the softening, if not erasing, of the stigma of poverty, as discussed previously. However, the introduction of sociological concepts into the public arena, not infrequently in a distorted manner, had the exact opposite effect, as we shall presently see.

With its new perspective on the nature of social ills such as poverty, social work reverted to its pre-World War I source of sociology, from which, to a great extent, it was hoped that an understanding of the problems and means for their alleviation and solution might be derived.[19] Social workers became, to many, the engineers and technologists who derive their knowledge and techniques from "applied sociology" (see Gouldner & Miller, 1972). A very important effect of this was to raise the status of sociology in the public mind. Sociology was no longer an esoteric, "ivory tower" discipline; it now became *the* discipline from which understanding and solutions to major social problems would flow.

It is precisely because of the perceived prominence of sociology in the area of social welfare policy formulation, that a number of its concepts have become the source of very emotion-laden controversies, and the concept of "the culture of poverty" is a case in point. We have seen that, actually, the concept has a long history in American sociology and, indeed, there is evidence that it is, to some extent, a useful concept. Yet some of its critics have charged that it is unsound because it involves value judgments; for example, the culture of poverty poor suffer from a "failure to strive sufficiently," "inability to communicate emotionally," "broken homes," "vicious environment," and, as Oscar Lewis (1966) summed it up "the poverty of culture is one of the crucial aspects of the culture of poverty." (p. lii; cf. Valentine, 1968). Other critics have even gone so far as to charge the culture of poverty theorists with being enemies of the poor

---

[19] It should be noted that some of the most prominent studies of poverty in the late 19th and early 20th centuries were sociologically oriented (cf. Charles Booth, 1902-3. 1910; Hunter, 1965; Pfautz, 1967.

(see Leacock, 1967; Ryan, 1971), and they have not been deterred by denials, such as that of Oscar Lewis (1967), who wrote that the culture of poverty "is an indictment not of the poor, but of the social system that produces the way of life...with its pathos and sufferering. It is also an indictment of some members of the middle class, government officials, and others who try to cover up the unpleasant and ugly facts of the culture of poverty" (p. 492). We would argue here that, in addition to our earlier criticism, while we do not question the intentions of the culture of poverty therorists, it is in the nature of the concept (as it is with a number of other sociological concepts) that it can and does serve as a stigma theory of the tribal type, especially after the very broad interpretation and wide publicity given to it, notably in Michael Harrington's best selling *The Other America* (1962). It can serve and has served in the past few years of general economic insecurity in the country as a rationale for curtailing welfare funds which in the mind of the public and played up in the mass media is the very source of our economic difficulties. In one week in the spring of 1970, *Time, Newsweek*, and *U.S. News and World Reports* all had cover stories dealing with the economic crisis, and all three focused upon "the welfare mess," leaving the reader with the natural conclusion that the latter is the cause of the former. The argument usually runs that the welfare rolls are full of employables who are unemployed simply because, being part of the culture of poverty, they are lazy parasites, and that much of the remainder of the welfare rolls consists of women who, being part of the culture of poverty, have no morals (or, more generously, live by a different set of moral standards) and have flocks and flocks of illegitimate children so that they can collect more money from welfare. These beliefs are strengthened by the government officials and others who constantly stress the need to put employable welfare recipients to work of any kind. The fact that, according to the U.S. Department of Health, Education and Welfare (1971), "less than one percent of Welfare recipients are able-bodied unemployed males," that "[t]he typical welfare family has a mother and three children," and that "[t]he average welfare family has been on the rolls for 23 months," falls on deaf ears is because "everybody knows" that there is a culture of poverty and that the vast amounts of money spent on welfare only help to perpetuate that culture. Again, we are not at all suggesting that the culture of poverty theorists subscribe to these myths, nor do we reject the concept on the grounds that it can and has been used by those who wish to reinforce these myths. What we do wish to illustrate is the manner in which social scientific concepts can serve as stigma theories, justifying the "varieties of discriminations" that we utilize to reduce the "life chances" of the poor.

RESPONSES TO STIGMA

Goffman maintains that stigmatized individuals share many problems and utilize common strategies to meet these problems. He discusses three options open to them by means of which they avoid interacting with "normals" under situations where they are at a disadvantage. One possibility is to associate only with those who possess the same stigma as themselves and, therefore, do not derogate them for it, or to associate only with those "normals" who are sympathetic, in the sense that for them the stigma is of no consequence. A second possibility is for the stigmatized individual to hide his identity as stigmatized, to pass (the extent to which this is possible depends, "obviously," on the nature of the stigma). A third possibility is that of "managing" the "audience" by playing on the meanings that "normals" give to his condition (1963b, pp. 9 ff).

Throughout his analysis, Goffman deals on the primary level with stigma and the reactions to it, both by "normals" and by the stigmatized; that is, the adjustments to stigma are individual reactions. Whereas his analysis is essentially microsociological, it is our contention that a more complete understanding of the nature of stigma can be derived if we were to analyze it macrosociologically. We would argue that just as the reaction of normals to stigma must be understood within "a language of relationships," within the societally established "means of categorizing persons and the complement of attributes felt to be ordinary and natural for members of each of these categories" (p. 2), so too must the reactions of the stigmatized individuals be understood within the context of culturally derived techniques of adjustment to situations where the stigmatized individual is interacting under a disadvantage. Goffman analyzes this within the context of the solitary individual, and suggests that the behavior of the stigmatized individual is, to a great extent, a self-fulfilling prophecy in the sense that the person having a stigma very often adjusts to the role prescriptions of how an individual with that stigma is supposed to behave and to what the society thinks of the individual with that particular stigma. It is argued here that *groups* of people may collectively derive techniques of adjusting to their situation of stigma, and that these collectively derived techniques will vary in accordance with the discussion in Chapter 3 of types of subcultures. Again, Weber's discussion of "style of life" is relevant.

One of the subcultures discussed in Chapter 3 was a "minority subculture," which may persist as the result of internal pressures to retain the group's unique norms and values, or may persist as the result of external pressures—that is, restrictions and barriers placed upon the minority group by the dominant group. Very often, it was stated, it persists as the result of both internal and external pressures, with either the external pressures leading to internal ones, or vice versa. When there are present external pressures, restrictions, and barriers, then there is present in that society what Weber calls "status segregation grown into caste," and "the caste structure transforms the horizontal and unconnected coexistences of ethnically segregated groups into a vertical social system of super- and subordination" (Weber, 1968, Vol. 2, p. 934). The reaction of the stigmatized subordinate caste may be to reject the status-honor system of the dominant group and maintain its own system where it has the most honor and the dominant group the least. Again, Weber observed that "even pariah peoples who are most despised (for example, the Jews) are usually apt to continue cultivating the belief in their own specific honor" (p. 934). The American Black Muslim group is (or was) an interesting example of this type of subculture; thus, it adopted a different status-honor system in reaction to and rejection of the dominant system in which it was stigmatized (see Essien-Udom, 1962; Lincoln, 1961).

Where the stigmatized group is an ethnic minority, the fact that it is a more or less homogeneous group makes it considerably more likely that that group will develop and retain its own unique status-honor and value system as a reaction to the stigma. When, however, the stigmatized group is an economic unit, rather than an ethnic unit, unless that lower economic class can "unite" to the point where it is in the position to reject the existing economic and value system and replace it with another, it will have to seek other means for adjusting to the situation of stigma. Or, to take an example of a group stigmatized because of physical stigma deformities, such as the blind or otherwise physically handicapped, they may be able to unite around the handicap in an effort to demonstrate that they are, in reality, not inferior to the nonhandicapped and do, in fact, possess certain qualities which deem them better suited to certain positions than the nonhandicapped (see TenBroek & Matson, 1959).

It is now possible to suggest an explanation of the different reactions to the stigma of poverty on the part of the heterogeneous members of the lower class as compared to that of a homogeneous lower class ethnic minority. The lower class ethnic or religious minority will, very often, as Weber pointed out, develop an alternative status-honor system of reference and will not live up to the expectations and images deriving from the dominant status-honor system. However, with a heterogeneous lower class—that is, a lower class which does not share a common positive ethnic and/or religious heritage and identity or a common physical characteristic—there is little basis from which may be formed an alternative system of status-honor with which the members of the lower class can identify. It is under those conditions that the reactions to the stigma of poverty are likely to result in a cluster of traits that have been described as the culture of poverty, which is not an independent culture nor a completely self-perpetuating subculture, but rather a quasiculture, *a dependent subculture*, in the sense that the persistence of the subculture is dependent upon the persistence of the stigma.[20]

To clarify what is meant by a "dependent subculture," it will be worthwhile to look at Robert K. Merton's (1968) discussion of the "self-fulfilling prophecy." As Merton describes it:

> The self-fulfilling prophecy is, in the beginning, a *false* definition of the situation evoking a new behavior which makes the originally false conception come *true*. The specious validity of the self-fulfilling prophecy perpetuates a reign of error. For the prophet will cite the actual course of events as proof that he was right from the very beginning. (p. 47, emphasis in original)

Merton builds his analysis upon W. I. Thomas' theorem: "If men define situations as real, they are real in their consequences." Surprisingly, Merton makes no reference to Charles Horton Cooley, whose concept of the "looking-glass self" is crucial for understanding why there develops the new behavior which now confirms the originally false definition of the situation; it develops because this is the self which, though false, is reflected in the looking-glass. It is, in the terminology of George Herbert Mead, the "me"—the role which he "takes" from the "others." It becomes a

---

[20] With this in mind, we should now reexamine the relationship between social class and values in the United States. It was shown in Chapter 3 that there is a difference in the priority on values between the lower class and the middle class. Oscar Lewis mentions as one of the characteristics of the "culture of poverty" that of "time orientation" which is different from that of those not in the "culture of poverty," certainly different from the time orientation of the non-poor. The poor, it is alleged, are present oriented, whereas the non-poor are future oriented. The basic question is, however, whether the different patterns manifested are the products of different values with reference to time orientation. S. M. Miller, F. Reissman, and A. A. Seagull (1968) in their article, "Poverty and Self-Indulgence: A critique of the Non-Deferred Gratification Pattern," have seriously questioned the assertion that the different spending patterns are the results of very different values with reference to time orientation. This and similar questions of this nature have been raised earlier (Chapter 3). What is of concern at this point is not the norms and values of the poor, but rather those of the middle class in America. To what extent is the behavior of the middle class the product of a middle class value system, and to what extent is this value system so strong that it is self-perpetuating? Is the middle class as future oriented, as deferred gratification oriented as has been alleged and accepted? If that were indeed the case, how would one explain the success of Master Charge, Bank Americard and numerous other credit card companies, the underlying theme of which is not to defer—"Buy now, pay later!" That the credit cards, with their plans for "extended payments" have so rapidly risen to the point where they almost replace the daily use of money and present a formidable challenge to savings banks, must raise serious questions about the middle class values which are so radically different from those of the lower class! This is not meant to suggest that there are no differences in values between the middle and lower classes, nor that values have no effect on behavior patterns. Rather, it is intended to demonstrate that the relationship between norms and values among classes as well as in societies in general is not clear and straightforward as it is often presented.

self-fulfilling prophecy because this is the only conception of self provided by the "looking-glass," "the other," and it is only with this conception of self that interaction of any kind with the "other" is possible. Furthermore, it becomes a vicious circle, or a "reign of error," because this self-perception and technique of adjustment to the situation of stigma is internalized and most often, though not exclusively, passed on intergenerationally through socialization. This is not to say that the techniques of adjustment to stigma are passed on as valued patterns, in the ideal sense; the ideal, obviously, would be not being stigmatized. But, so long as the situation of stigma exists, the patterns of adjustment to it are transmitted through socialization.

When the stigmatized group is an ethnic or religious minority, then its own self-image derived from its own system of values and status-honor may serve as its looking-glass, the "other," from which the members derive their social selves. They have their own positive reference group. On the other hand, when the lower class is heterogeneous and many members do not have a common alternative status-honor system and a system of values deriving from a common ethnic heritage, then they are more likely to internalize the "spoiled identity" which the stigma casts upon them,

---

The question of the relationship between norms and values among social classes within a particular society is similar to the broader question of the relationship between ideas and institutions in total societies. A rigid ("vulgar") Marxist position maintains that it is economic substructure which *determines* superstructure of which ideas and values are a basic element. This position would extend the determinative power of the economic substructure to the behavior of individuals as well. On the other hand, a similarly vulgar Weberian position would assert that it is solely ideas which determine the social structure of the society. That Weber himself did not adhere to this position is indicated by his statement at the conclusion of *The Protestant Ethic and the Spirit of Capitalism*: "it is...not my aim to substitute for a one-sided materialistic an equally one-sided spiritualistic causal interpretation of culture and history" (1958, p. 183.) Norman Birnbaum (1953), in his article "Conflicting Interpretations of the Rise of Capitalism: Marx and Weber," argues that, likewise, neither was Marx a wholly economic determinist, and that with respect to the social action of individuals, in particular, Marx recognized the importance of motivation (pp. 129-132). Marx's rejection of the vulgarization of his theory was expressed, says Birnbaum, in his own observation that, "Je ne suis pas Marxiste."

A theory which stresses the need to recognize the importance of both ideas and social structure, and the reciprocal relationship between them, is to be found in the writings of Peter L. Berger, (Berger, 1967; Berger & Luckmann, 1966). Whereas Berger deals primarily with the reciprocal relationship between individual and society (he consistently calls it a "dialectical" relationship), the similarly reciprocal relationship between ideas and social structure follows quite naturally from his analysis of the three steps in the "dialectical" process, "externalization, objectivation, and internalization" (1967), pp. 3-26). In brief, society is a world-building enterprise. Man pours out meaning onto society, these meanings become "objectivated," that is, they attain the quality of objective reality, and they are then internalized in the structures of the subjective consciousness of the individual. Once this ongoing process is recognized, it then becomes evident that with respect to the relationship between ideas and social structure, a one-sided monocausal position is untenable because, by their very nature, ideas and social structure can only be related in a reciprocal manner.

and the reign of error, the self-fulfilling prophecy is then set in motion, producing a dependent subculture.

Having seen the long history and depth of the stigma of poverty in the United States and hypothesizing the process of adjustment to the situation of stigma, what emerges is a much clearer picture of the meaning of the stigma to the poor and a clearer understanding of the significance and meaning of the patterns of behavior and attitudes forming the cluster of traits discussed earlier.

On the matter of the relationship between poverty and crime in the United States, the questions raised by the Landers and the evidence presented by Rosenberg and Silverstein, discussed in the beginning of Chapter 2, suggest that the poor have not internalized the goal of success, as maintained by Merton (1938) in this theory of "Social Structure and Anomie." On the contrary, the isolation of the poor produced by the stigma of poverty continuously insures that the poor will not internalize this goal. As far as Merton's assertion that the goals are "held to transcend class lines," this does not mean that they are so held by the poor. It is the non-poor who maintain that they *should* transcend class lines, at the same time that they are insuring by the stigma that the goals will not transcend class lines. That this is somewhat of a contradiction on the part of the non-poor is, of course, true but not unique. It is somewhat analgous to the contradiction in American culture which Gunnar Myrdal (1964) focuses upon in his study of *An American Dilemma*. That it is not applicable to the lower class does not mean that Merton is basically incorrect when he says that the disproportionate emphasis upon success generates deviant and criminal behavior. On the contrary, his is quite possibly a very accurate explanation of organized crime and white-collar crime (cf. Bell, 1962, especially Chapter 7, "Crime as an American Way of Life"). And it is precisely because of the application of Merton's theory to organized and white-collar crime that Rodman (1962) is somewhat misleading when he asserts that "the members of the lower class...have a wider range of values than others within the society" (p. 209), because what white-collar crime illustrates is that the middle class too stretches its values in many cases. Likewise, the middle class develops what Matza (1964) calls "techniques of neutralization," (p. 176), when it commits white-collar crimes, as has been demonstrated by Donald R. Cressey (1970) in his study on the social psychology of embezzlement.

What neither the culturalists nor the situationalists have considered is the possibility that one of the harshest effects of the stigma of poverty is that it results in the isolation of the poor from not only the material provisions of the society, but also, and perhaps equally important, from the cultural provisions as well. It is from the society and its culture that each member receives his social self, his sense of identity and self-identification, and it is only when the individual is part of the society and identifies with it that he internalizes its normative system, its values, and its definitions of reality. Therefore, the stigmatized and isolated poor of the society, unless they have a different cultural system with which they identify and which they internalize (as is the case with some minority subcultures), do not internalize the structures of a society as do those who are truly part of the society. Their "me" is quite different in nature from that of the real members of society. They do not completely internalize the normative system of society. This does not mean that they are unaware of the norms and values of society. They are very much aware of them, but these have not become part of their subjective consciences to the extent that they adhere to them because they really believe in them.

Thus, the structuralists are incorrect because they maintain that the poor adhere to the society's values as intensely as do the non-poor, but that it is the restrictive social structure which results in their non-conforming behavior. The culturalists, on the other hand, maintain that the poor have a basically different value system from that of the non-poor. In both cases, there is the assertion that the poor have a complete cultural system; the only question is whether it is that of the dominant society—the structuralist position—or an alternate system—the cultural position. What is being asserted here is that, as the result of the stigmatization and isolation of the poor, there is a somewhat less than successful internalization of any cultural system.

Since the cultural system has not been fully internalized and does not fully mold the subjective conscience according to its dictates, the individual must develop his sense of identity through his own experiences. The society has not provided him, as it has for those who are intrinsic members, an almost ready-made identity through the socialization process. His "real me" is the existential me. He is not trying to "make it"; he is always "getting by," and the higher crime rate in the lower class is one of the collectively developed techniques for getting by. Likewise, in school, he is biding his time, getting by, and in this situation it is even more than usually obvious because in the school situation the stigmatization is even more manifest. And it may not be too farfetched to suggest that this stigmatization and the effects discussed may be one of the sources of the higher rate of schizophrenia among members of the lower class.

Gerald D. Suttles has pointed out another invidious aspect of slum life, which he terms "differential moral isolation," and which we would include under the effects of the stigma of poverty. According to Suttles (1968):

> In all societies there are probably people who fall short of existing standards that attest to their trustworthiness and self-restraint. The standards of American society are severe, and a very

> large proportion of our population is regarded with suspicion and caution. Typically, these are poor people from a low-status minority group and unable to manage very well their "public relations." The presence of such a group of people is disruptive because it undermines the trust residents must share to go about their daily rounds. In American society, a common solution to this difficulty has been to relegate all suspicious people to "slums" and "skid rows." As a result, respectable and essential citizens can carry on their corporate life undisturbed by their apprehensions.
>
> Slum residents, however, are subject to all the suspicions and bear those disreputable characteristics that turn people away from one another and interfere with joint activities. Seen from the standpoint of the wider community, slum residents do not inspire levels of trust necessary to the usual round of neighborhood activities. Out of necessity, then, they may fall back on local patterns which guarantee their safety and promote association. (pp. 5-6)

Moreover, Suttles finds that the moral system which develops in the slum is much more personalistic than in the larger society.

> The social order that emerges...does not consist of a series of highly standardized role capacities. Addams area residents relate to one another primarily by a personalistic morality in which individual precedent is the major standard for evaluation. The most incongruous of people become associated and continue to remain safe companions. Judgments of worth and social sanctions are individuated and tailored to past commitments. Normative rulings, then, do not apply to a fixed role apart from the incumbent; they can be developed only as individuals have the time and occasion to become familiar with each others' past history and future intentions. (pp. 228-229)

This personalistic moral system cannot be accounted for either by the cultural or situational perspectives, but is readily understandable when we view the relationship between the slum residents and the larger society.

In terms of explanation, both the cultural and situational perspectives have been found to be inadequate. Viewed in isolation, the cluster of traits appear to be self-perpetuating, because they are internalized and transmitted through socialization. But this subcultural view is deceptive because it ignores the interaction of the poor with the non-poor—that is, it ignores the stigma of poverty which sets the process into motion, and prevents that process from being broken *so long as the stigma persists.* On the other hand, it is to distort the effects of the stigma to maintain, as do a number of situationalists, that the patterns and attitudes are not internalized, that they are "thinner and less weighty" (Liebow, 1967, p. 213, n.3) and that they would rapidly disappear with a change in the situation. That this is not the case can be shown from the experience of one of the central characters in Liebow's own study. Liebow recounts that Richard did not take advantage of a job opportunity because he feared the responsibilities involved, and he "knew" that he would fail. He "knew" that he would fail because he had repeatedly experienced failure. He had been conditioned; he internalized this image of himself and of society (pp. 54-56). This condition is precisely the one to which Oscar Lewis (1966) was referring when he wrote that the culture-of-poverty poor may not be "psychologically geared to take full advantage of changing conditions or increased opportunities which may occur in their lifetime" (p. xlv). It must be added and emphasized (and it will be discussed in the next chapter) that the situation is determined not only by conditions and opportunities, in their own right, but also by the interpretations given to them by both the poor and the non-poor, and this is inexorably linked with the stigma of poverty.

It is the perspective of this analysis, then, that the persistence of poverty and the behavior of the poor cannot be attributed to solely internal nor external sources. Rather, they have both internal and external sources which are reciprocally related, in that the patterns and attitudes of the poor are adjustments to the stigma of poverty, and these adjustments are transmitted intergenerationally through socialization. Socialization, the internal aspect, teaches the young how to behave in situations of stress, which are the product of the external aspect, the stigma of poverty.

Having rejected both the situational and cultural explanations and having suggested earlier that one of the major sources of the controversy over the subject during the 1960s was the implicit and explicit policy implications which derive from these contrasting positions, and that the failure of policy may be in part that it rested upon an inadequate explanation, the next chapter turns to the policy implications of the "relational" perspective developed here. The objective will not be to formulate a panacea, nor even any specific program or group of programs. Rather, it will be shown that the relational perspective can serve as a criterion in the evaluation of social policy in that it suggests the direction which any "successful" policy must take.

Chapter 5

FROM ISOLATION TO INTEGRATION: AN INDEX FOR THE EVALUATION OF SOCIAL POLICY

With the professionalization of the social sciences in America in recent decades, there has arisen the notion that the "acid test" of an analysis is its relevance for "applied sociology." Many Americans, professional sociologists and laymen alike, have come to expect that an analysis of a sociological phenomenon, and particularly a social problem, will be shown to have implications for altering that phenomenon, for "solving" that social problem. While this is a notion with which we do not necessarily concur, we do feel that the analysis of the stigma of poverty which has been presented does lend itself to the derivation of implications for social policy. If the source of the problem of the "cluster of poverty traits" which has come to be termed "the culture of poverty" lies in the stigma of poverty, then the crucial question in terms of the "solution" to that "problem" is, how can that stigma be removed, erased, or at least significantly alleviated? It is toward this question that this chapter turns, and a number of hypothetical and realistic possibilities will be explored.

In the notes to the previous chapter, reference was made to the question of the relationship between values and social structure, superstructure, and infrastructure, with the rigid Marxists arguing that social structure determines values and the rigid Weberians arguing that values determine social structure. Without agreeing with either of these contrasting positions, we shall proceed to analyze two types of approaches to the problem of alleviating the stigma of poverty, one which is termed an "absolute" approach and the other a "relative" approach. Within each approach, the possibilities of affecting change in both values and social structure will be examined.

The first hypothetical possibility in an absolute approach to the alleviation of the stigma of poverty would call for a major overhaul in the American value structure to the point that poverty would be converted from stigma to virtue. Using a powerful dose of sociological imagination, let it be envisioned that the government would now proclaim that poverty is a virtue and the poor are the most worthy. This was, after all, the case among the post-exilic Hebrews and early Christians, as was noted above. In more recent times, these were the values of the pioneers of the kibbutz movement in Israel. According to Yonina Talmon (1972), "[a]cceptance of the bitter poverty which was the laborer's lot in those days was a decisive test of solidarity. A life of poverty also served as a badge of distinction for the select group of those who were actively involved in the realization of the goal" (p. 207). This is an absolute approach because it calls for a total revolution in the values of American society. But would it work? If achieved, it would by definition mean the end of the stigma of poverty. The problem is, however, that even if it could be imagined that the government of the United States would proclaim that to be poor would henceforth be deemed a virtue, it is more than doubtful that these values would be realized in the society. The individualistic ideology is so thoroughly rooted in the American culture that it is inconceivable that these could be drastically changed voluntarily.[21] Moreover, while it is true that poverty was a mark of distinction among the pioneers of the kibbutz movement, even the kibbutz with its strong collectivist ideology was not long in abandoning this value (Talmon, 1972, pp. 208ff). In any case, the kibbutz is less than four percent of Israeli society, and is in many ways dependent upon the non-collectivist majority. To imagine such values in American society is to engage in social science fiction.

An alternative absolute approach could be one that is directed at a basic social structural change. Since the stigma of poverty is internalized because of a lack of real or perceived alternatives, and since it is the political structure which supports the exploiting and restricting economic and social structures, it might be suggested that revolution is an effective means of breaking the stigma of poverty. Moreover, from the context of the poor themselves, a revolutionary ideology might just provide that alternative system of goals and values which might help them to prevent the persistence of the vicious cycle and to cast off the effects of the stigma. It is interesting to note that this is the very solution which Oscar Lewis (1966) saw for the "culture of poverty" in underdeveloped countries,

> where great masses live in the culture of poverty.... In these countries the people with a culture of poverty may seek a more revolutionary solution. By creating structural changes in society,

[21] It should be noted that the rejection of the individualistic ideology has been one of driving forces behind a number of attempts at counterculture communes. It is difficult to envision, however, that these would have any significant impact upon the value structure of American society as a whole.

> by redistributing wealth, by organizing the poor and giving them a sense of belonging, of power and of leadership, revolutions frequently succeed in abolishing some of the basic characteristics of the culture of poverty. (p. lii)

And after embarking on his last major study in Cuba, Lewis wrote:

> I have just returned from a six month stay in Cuba, which is the first lap of an ambitious three year research project on the revolutionary process and its effects on family life, etc....I am...convinced that the Cubans have already eliminated the major conditions which breed the sub-culture of poverty. Where the sub-culture of poverty continues to persist in Cuba, it is a carry-over from pre-revolutionary conditions. (personal communication, Sept. 15, 1969)

But Lewis himself did not suggest a revolution for the elimination of the culture of poverty in the United States. He distinguished between those countries, such as the United States, in which the culture of poverty "represents a relatively small segment of the population and those in which it constitutes a very large one.Obviously the solutions will differ in these two situations" (1966, p. lii). The fact, however, that Lewis did not advocate revolution as a means for eliminating the culture of poverty in the United States tells us more about his political ideologies than it does about the effectiveness of revolution as a means for breaking the stigma of poverty in the United States.

On the other hand, it would appear that Lewis had overrated the effectiveness of revolution even in underdeveloped countries. Take, for example, the end of the last sentence in the passage from *La Vida* just quoted. Lewis claimed that revolutions frequently do achieve the elimination of the culture of poverty, "even when they do not succeed in abolishing poverty itself." If they, the revolutions, do not succeed in abolishing poverty, then it remains to be seen whether, in fact, the absence of the culture of poverty is permanent or only temporary. In other words, it may be that the revolutionary ideology only provides a camouflage or a breathing spell to the culture of poverty, but that once the ideological passions cool somewhat, the culture of poverty will reassert itself. And Lewis' trip to Cuba taught him, he said, that it is much more difficult to abolish poverty in these (underdeveloped) countries than he had earlier anticipated (personal communication, Sept. 15, 1969). As for the United States, besides the fact that the chances for revolution are, to say the least, very remote, unless the revolutionary ideology were widespread throughout the society and the revolution were a complete success, it may be predicted that the stigma of poverty would soon reassert itself.

In any case, revolution is beyond the boundaries of social policy, since social policy relates to the whole gamut of social services under government administration.[22] While it is therefore true that social policy is thus *ipso facto* conservative (that is, it is based on the political *status quo*), this does not invalidate the drawing of conclusions for social policy from sociological analysis. If this is the stated objective, then obviously revolution is beyond the realm of conclusions to be drawn from the study. Since this chapter seeks to derive from the preceding analysis an index for the evaluation of social policy, it will concentrate on relative rather than absolute approaches to the elimination of the stigma of poverty.

In one of his controversial statements on the relationship between social science and social policy, Daniel Patrick Moynihan (1969) emphatically maintained that. "[t]*he role of social science lies not in the formulation of social policy, but in the measurement of its results*" (p. 193, emphasis in original).

As stated, this is a position with which we would strongly disagree if for no other reason than that a sound evaluation of social policy must implicitly, if not explicitly, contain suggestions for the formulation of policy. If the evaluation is negative, then it at least implies that the direction of policy must be changed and it would suggest the direction of change. If the evaluation is positive, then it is assisting in the formulation of policy along those lines. Furthermore, implicit in every evaluation is a notion of what the situation should be, and that is the standard by which the policies are evaluated. While the precise relationship between the stigma of poverty and the "culture of poverty" remains to be explored and verified, the relational perspective suggested offers the possibility of developing and implementing new directions in social welfare policy which may reduce the pragmatic importance of the whole issue, if not render it moot altogether. The policy direction that we shall recommend calls for basic situational change which aims at the *relational* problem—the problem of the relationship between the poor and the non-poor.

Since the foregoing analysis has *suggested* the stigma of poverty as a crucial variable in explaining the persistence of the cluster of traits associated with poverty, the "culture of poverty," it should now be possible to account to some extent for the failure of America's social welfare policies

[22] Our conception of social policy has been influenced by T. H. Marshall and Richard M. Titmuss. Marshall sees it referring "to the policy of governments with regard to action having a direct impact on the welfare of the citizens, by providing them with services or income. The central core consists, therefore, of social insurance, public (or national) assistance, the health and welfare services, and housing policy" (Marshall, 1965, p. 7). Titmuss has a broader conception of social policy which involves the direct public provision of services and benefits, and also fiscal and occupational welfare (Titmuss, 1968, p. 192). Both Marshall and Titmuss see social policy within the context of government action (cf. Titmuss, 1974, p. 24).

as being rooted in an incomplete understanding of poverty and its effects. When we examine these policies, we find that they are based on either a cultural or a situational perspective, but there has been no social welfare policy that has been based upon the relational perspective. We shall look, for example, at the Economic Opportunity Act of 1964 and a number of its components, and find that the Act as a unit was not based entirely on either one of the two perspectives. Rather, some components were based on a cultural perspective and others were based on a situational one. None of the components appears to have been very successful, and it is now possible to attribute the lack of success, *in part,* to the fallacies which inhere in the theoretical frameworks. It is emphasized that this was only part of the problem, though a major one. There were other problems, some of which will be cited, which may have, in any case, rendered the goals of the programs unachievable.

The early 1960s emphasized community organization and the involvement of the poor in programs on their own behalf as an effective and essential method of fighting poverty and its effects. According to its advocates, this approach is based upon the rejection of the cultural explanation and the acceptance, instead, of the situational one. For example, because of the successes of The Woodlawn Organization (TWO) in community organization, Warren C. Haggstrom (1968) cautions that

> when a scientist observes that a group of persons, the poor, have adopted their own patterns of behavior and system of belief, this does not mean that the behavior and belief patterns are cultural or that these patterns represent durable characteristics of the people involved over a wide variety of social situations. These patterns and beliefs may be situational, not internalized, and may shift readily as the situation changes. (p. 119)

He concludes that the basic problem is one of powerlessness, and to overcome this "powerful conflict organizations based in neighborhoods of poverty" are needed (p. 134). Haggstrom and others based their "solutions" on a limited conflict-theory approach, which, as shall be seen, overestimated the ability of the poor to engage in protracted conflict with the non-poor.

It was stated in Chapter 4 that the theoretical framework of the Community Action Program (CAP) component of the Economic Opportunity Act of 1964 had its roots in juvenile delinquency theory. To see this, let us recall the basic disagreement reviewed in Chapter 2 between Walter Miller and Cloward and Ohlin over the explanation of lower class delinquency. Miller saw lower class delinquency as a product of lower class culture; Cloward and Ohlin saw it as resulting from the lower class youth's awareness of his limited opportunity to achieve the conventional forms of success. Cloward and Ohlin reject the notion of lower class culture; the crux of the problem, to them, is that of opportunity. Accordingly, to Cloward and Ohlin (the situationalists), a policy aimed at the reduction of lower class delinquency must be one that increases legitimate opportunities for lower class youth. This was the theme of their Mobilization For Youth program, and they were most influential in incorporating the CAP component into the "war on poverty." (Cf. Donovan 1967; Marris & Rein, 1967; Moynihan, 1969; Rubin, 1967.) CAP's explicit repudiation of Miller and his cultural perspective is attested to by Moynihan:

> Obviously Miller would not do....However scientifically sound, Miller appeared to be politically conservative, and therefore, one is led to suspect, did not meet the needs of the private agenda of the middle class reformers, namely, to prove a case against middle class society. (1969, p. 172)

Parenthetically, it is thus somewhat amusing to find Valentine (1968), owing to his rejection of the subcultural perspective, chiding Oscar Lewis for being so influential in devising the anti-poverty program: "It is most unfortunate that the poverty-culture idea should be so influential in public policy as a factor supporting bias in one ideological direction" (p. 70). In a review of Valentine's book, Lewis (1969) retorts:

> At one point Valentine charges that my concept of a culture of poverty was a guiding principle of the War Against Poverty and must, therefore, bear some responsibility for its failure. What a naive and absurd conception of the power of social science in our society! It is not the concept of a culture or subculture of poverty which is responsible for the lack of success of the anti-poverty program, but rather (1) the failure of the President and the Congress of the United States to understand the degree of national commitment necessary to cope with the problems; and (2) the Vietnam war, which has been draining our economic and human resources. (p. 6)

We would disagree with both Valentine and Lewis in this argument. As for Valentine, we have provided evidence that it was not the "poverty-culture" idea but the situational one which was the basis of at least the CAP component of the anti-poverty program. As for Lewis, while we would not take issue with his two points, we believe that he underestimated the extent to which social scientists were influential in devising the anti-poverty program. It just so happened that they were social scientists who adhered to the situational, rather than to his cultural, explanation.

In contrast to Valentine, Kenneth B. Clark attributes the very failure of the Community Action Program to its "naive" rejection of the culture of poverty. As he puts it (United States Senate, 1967), one factor

> which I think is responsible for the actual ineffectiveness of antipoverty programs as a means of changing basically the predicament of people in our slums, was reliance in the role of the indigenous, the maximum feasible participation of the poor approach.... Those of us who were involved in setting up the prototype of these programs I think were somewhat naive and sentimental. We did not take into account the effect of poverty and deprivation on the human personality. We did not calculate that for the poor the chief consequence of the culture of poverty is a kind of human stagnation, acceptance, defeat, which made meaningful involvement of the poor more verbal than real. (p. 2759)

As to the alleged successes of Alinsky-styled organizing programs, to which Haggstrom referred, Clark (Clark & Hopkins, 1970) suggests that "there is...no evidence that the Alinsky approach, in spite of the extensive publicity and success in a few skirmishes with power groups, has contributed to any observable changes of real significance in the basic conditions of the poor in those communities in which he has worked" (p. 253). A similar conclusion is drawn by Frank Riessman (1967), who finds that, "in essence, Alinsky's approach represents tactics without strategy, protest without a program" (p. 477; see also Riessman, 1965).

Whereas CAP was formulated from a situational perspective, the Operation Head Start component of the Economic Opportunity Act was thoroughly grounded in the subcultural perspective. In Chapter 2 we discussed the cultural and situational explanations of the problems which the poor confront in school; Deutch saw the problem as a cultural one, while Clark saw it as situational—educational deprivation. Proponents of both approaches agreed that Head Start was based upon the cultural perspective and thus had very different anticipations as to its success or failure. Among those anticipating the success of Head Start was J. McVicker Hunt, whom we quoted at the end of Chapter 1.

On the other hand, the structuralist or situational adaptationalist was, from the beginning, skeptical of the effects which Head Start might have. For example, Robert A. Dentler (1967) after examining the plans and proposals of the educational components of community action programs in four Eastern cities, declares:

> The main impression I get from a reading of the educational programs proposed, and in part acted upon...is a sense of their *limited scope* and *institutional superficiality*. Indeed...I believe we

> cannot call these programs in the domain of public education innovations at all...[o]ne finds in the planning of educational projects in the four community development programs under consideration, *no earmarks of citizen participation.* (pp. 159, 161, emphasis in original.

So long as there is no basic institutional change and citizen participation, the situationalist would not expect the programs to succeed.

As it turned out, after the program was in operation for several years, there was little disagreement that Head Start did not live up to the hopes of its supporters. The United States Commission on Civil Rights (1967) reported that, "[t]he fact remains...that none of the programs appears to have significantly raised achievement of participating pupils, as a group, within the period of evaluation by the Commission" (p. 138). To the situationalist, this came as no surprise, for he never had any faith in a program that was not aimed at altering the basic educational institution. The culturalist, on the other hand, typically attributed the failure of the program not to any theoretical deficiency but rather to its mechanics and operational inadequacies. Hunt (1969), for example, who was so optimistic that Head Start would achieve its goals, attributes its failure to the fact that "the various kinds of curricula from the traditional nursery school were employed in the school of Head Start, sometimes quite inexpertly by teachers accustomed to older children (p. 217). And, he says, Head Start is not the whole story of compensatory education. "Compensatory educational programs have existed outside Project Head Start...Gains of considerable magnitude in several programs, approaching 30 points in I.Q. during the course of a year, have been reported in programs of compensatory education which differ in curriculum and in method of teaching substantially" (p. 218). To Hunt, the failure of Head Start lies in the operational inadequacies which did not allow the program to provide the sufficient cultural and educational "enrichment" necessary to overcome the disadvantages facing the child.

As was mentioned at the conclusion of Chapter 1, Job Corps was based upon a cultural perspective. The fact that after the training, the youth would invariably return to his "vicious environment," does not appear to have been given much attention. In any case, the cost became highly controversial, and the program died.

We suggested at the beginning of this chapter that the lack of success of the projects within the anti-poverty program was due to a number of problems, and we state now that these problems were of different dimensions. The first type of problem was one of logistics, stemming from the multidimensional manner in which the problem of poverty manifests itself. As we have seen, poverty involves not only lack of money, but also manifests itself in the areas of education, mental health, crime and delinquency, etc. The problem which immediately arises, then, is that the "specialist" in each discipline is likely to emphasize the need for programs in his particular area, with priority over programs in other areas. An educator will emphasize educational programs, a mental health specialist will emphasize mental health programs, etc. This emphasis tends to blind each "specialist" to other programs in other areas. The limitations on resources for funds and the resultant competition for funds enhance this tendency for each to push his program, often by denigrating others. As a result, even the most theoretically sound project within a specific program is not likely to reap much success unless it is combined with others in other areas within a comprehensive, well-coordinated program. In fact, what happened with Head Start was that it was run almost entirely by educators within the traditional education system and was treated as a separate entity with almost no coordination with other programs (see Waxman, 1968, p. xiv). Much of the failure to coordinate the various programs within the Economic Opportunity Act must be, and has been, laid at the door of the Office of Economic Opportunity, which was the agency created specifically for coordinating those programs. As Sar A. Levitan (1969) asserts, "If OEO is viewed as a coordinating agency...its record must be viewed with skepticism" (p. 57).

During the late 1960s there were a number of instances of advocating "programs" with such zealousness that one can only surmise that their advocates were such "true believers," in the Eric Hoffer sense, that they became totally desensitized to the deleterious effects that their actions could, and did, have. For example, a number of years ago a group of social scientists came to the conclusion that the New York City public school system needed major overhauling, that the educational problems of the poor (specifically, the black poor) were the result of the failure of the schools, that these poor were "powerless" to effect any changes in a system controlled by (white) non-poor professional educators and politicians. To solve this problem, they advocated what to them was the only logical conclusion and plan—"community control" of the schools, whereby the school board would be made up of representatives of the "community" ("the people"), and its immediate goals would be to abolish the "racist" merit system and to insure that the teachers and curricula were "relevant" to the needs of the community (cf. Altshuler, 1970; Berube & Gittell, 1969; Gittell & Hevesi, 1969; Levin, 1970; Mayer, 1969; Wasserman, 1970). Aside from contributing to the New York City teachers' strike in the fall of 1968, and to a major split in the city in general along racial lines, the tragedy was that many, if not most, of the parents whose children were supposed to benefit from that community control were adamantly opposed to that particular form of community control. They wanted their children to be taught by what society-at-large recognizes as qualified teachers. Furthermore, there is no evidence that the "community" has fared any better in ridding the schools which they run of poor teachers and recruiting ones better than those already there. On the contrary, in testimony before a meeting of the Temporary State Charter Revision Commission for the City of New York, Dr. Kenneth Clark found the New York City experiment with community control to be "disastrous" (New York City, 1972):

> It is my considered judgment that the results of educational decentralization and community control have been disastrous and will be even more disastrous as we continue to say rationally, you know, we have too little time. My judgment that decentralization and community control of the public schools of New York City is disastrous is based on my concern as to what its initial purpose was, and let me admit before that that concern is probably quite unrealistic in terms of policy, in terms of race, in terms of, you know, white versus black and Jewish, black, etcetera, and I am willing to admit before you gentlemen ask your questions, that my judgment on the fact that decentralization of the public schools is a disaster and will continue to be a disaster is based upon the very limited standard of academic achievement of children, because that is the only concern I have. (pp. 1356-1357)

Moreover, and more to the point, by advocating and attempting to implement a too hastily conceived form of community control, what resulted is a hardening of the animosities which the (white) non-poor have for the (black) poor, serving only to harshen the dual stigma of race and poverty. In this case, it appears as if the social scientist was playing a dangerous game by experimenting with his "theories" at the expense of the poor. With the best of intentions, he was engaging in a form of Russian Roulette, with the gun aimed at his intended beneficiaries, not himself. To a great extent, this was the consequence of the social scientist's ignorance, or lack of awareness, of the relational character of poverty, the vicious circle which his actions could only make more vicious.

To see this problem even more clearly, let us look at some of the tactics and proposals to bring about welfare reform. Criticism of public assistance in America knows no political boundaries. Most social scientists agree that it contributes to the breakup of families and that there are many poor who are eligible for assistance but do not receive it, some because they are unaware of their eligibility, others who are aware but do not wish to be stigmatized, and still others who have been denied entrance onto or have been removed from the welfare rolls (cf. Cloward, 1966;

Cloward & Elman, 1966; Cloward & Piven, 1968; Elman, 1965; Krosney, 1966). Since the welfare system is a conglomeration of federal, state, and local legislation (see Elman, 1965, especially Chapter 1), and is beyond reform, Cloward and others have advocated the disruption of the welfare system. That is, they have advocated the organization of welfare recipients and potential recipients to demand the monies to which they are legally entitled. This would lead to the bankruptcy of city governments and would force the federal government to "dump" the welfare system and replace it with a more "humane" form of assistance, such as a guaranteed annual income. Cloward has gone so far as to help set up the Poverty/Welfare Rights organization, which is supposed to be a union of the organized poor. Differences in approach have subsequently developed between Cloward and the organization, now called NWRO (National Welfare Rights Organization). Cloward still retains his faith in the possibility of recruiting new welfare recipients, thereby flooding the rolls and bringing about the disruption, whereas NWRO, under the leadership of Dr. George Wiley,[23] concentrated on organizing those already on the rolls to insure that they get their just due. In any case, the crisis and bankruptcy have not ensued, at least not as the result of Cloward's doings. In New York for example, the city government rapidly removed one of the major leverage points of the strategy. Cloward and others had sought to bring on the disruption by having welfare recipients demand the special allotments to which they were entitled. For example, at the beginning of the school year, recipients could request and were entitled to a special allowance for school clothing for their children. This is just one of the many special allotments to which recipients were entitled, and of which many of them were unaware. Under the direction of a number of people at Columbia University's School of Social Work, a guide entitled "Your Rights on Welfare" was published and was to be distributed free of charge to all welfare recipients. This guide listed in complete detail the exact types of services and amounts of money to which each client is entitled. Had it been successful, this campaign would have most certainly pushed the city's budget, already hovering on the verge of crisis, over the brink. With unusual speed, New York changed its welfare laws and replaced the special allotments with a "simplified payments system," which meant that clients now received a flat grant, slightly increased from what it had been previously, and were now expected to take care of all their special needs from their regular allotments. Again, the intended beneficiaries were now worse off than they were before the intervention of their "benefactors."

---

[23] Dr. Wiley died by drowning in the Chesapeake Bay on August 8, 1973, at the age of 42.

What if Cloward's strategy of disruption had been successful? Suppose it did succeed in bankrupting cities; would this necessarily force the federal government to replace it with a more humane program? What, first of all, are the details of that program? Second, and more important, having seen how deeply rooted and all-pervasive the stigma of poverty is (see the Free & Cantril poll, 1968, discussed above) and especially with the very close association of welfare with blacks in the public mind, is it not reasonable to assume that the strategy would lead, not to a war on poverty but to a "war on the poor"? Once again, the "reign of error," the vicious circle of the stigma of poverty, had been overlooked.

In an effort to combat the family disorganizing effects of welfare, specifically Aid to Families with Dependent Children (AFDC), and in an effort to reduce the high cost of welfare and the wide variations in welfare allotments from state to state (which, allegedly, induces many poor to move from states with low allotments to those with higher ones—we say "allegedly" because the evidence indicates that the actual number of poor involved is quite small), President Nixon proposed a Welfare Reform bill, the Family Assistance Program (FAP). The story of this program has been detailed by its chief architect, Daniel Patrick Moynihan, in his book, *The Politics of a Guaranteed Income* (1973). As seen through Moynihan's account (which by its very nature is partisan—is there such a thing as an "objective" account?), he was very much aware of the form of arguments he could expect to encounter from his conservative opponents, and he mustered all of his political, intellectual, and theatrical talents to stave off the opposition. He set the stage by presenting the problem, not as one of *poverty* but as one of *dependency* (p. 17). It seems fair to assume that he presented the problem in this manner, not so much for the purpose of social scientific accuracy but rather to weaken the opposition to poverty programs, which Nixon had campaigned strongly against. Moreover, he ingeniously presented the program as a family assistance program rather than stating that it was a form of guaranteed income which combined Milton Friedman's idea of a negative income tax with a system of family allowances. In fact, President Nixon went so far as to emphatically declare that the Family Assistance Program was not a guaranteed income (p. 11), though it most certainly was.

This is not the place to review either the complexities and fate of FAP nor Moynihan's book. Certain aspects of the experience of FAP are, however, very relevant to the argument herein. Under this program (as initially presented; many amendments were subsequently added before it met its final fate), a family of four with an income of less than $1,000 annually would receive a minimum allotment of $1,600 annually. Furthermore, a working head of household would be able to retain the first $720 of his earnings, and 50% of his income above that amount, and still obtain assistance, providing his income did not go beyond the cutoff amount of $3,920. This latter provision was included for the expressed purpose of providing a work incentive, for the fear of many critics of welfare and welfare reform is that these programs encourage people not to work. As we saw in the discussion in Chapter 4, this was one of the major criticisms of the Speenhamland Act of 1795. The belief that welfare induces people not to work, and that there is virtue in work (at least for the next person) remains omnipresent. Whether or not there is substance to this belief is quite irrelevant, as the Thomas theorem makes clear. Furthermore, even with the work incentive, there was, according to Moynihan, opposition to FAP, particularly from Arthur Burns, then the President's economic advisor, who claimed it was simply another version of the ill-fated Speenhamland scheme. Burns' staff prepared a paper quoting Karl Polanyi's account of Speenhamland. To counter Burns' opposition, the Urban Affairs staff consulted with Gertrude Himmelfarb, who argued that, contrary to Polanyi, Speenhamland was not a disaster and, in any case, FAP was essentially different in that the recipient was not penalized dollar for dollar on his earnings up to cutoff line (Moynihan, 1973, pp. 179-180).

But the work incentive was not enough for Nixon's Cabinet. Most of the members of the Cabinet were opposed to FAP because it did not contain an explicit work *requirement.* President Nixon was not present at the heated debate, and when he heard of the work requirement hangup, his response was purely pragmatic. "I don't care a damn about the work requirements," declared the President. "This is the price of getting $1,600" (Moynihan, 1973, pp. 218-220). Ironically, this pragmatic gesture was to no avail, and Nixon and Moynihan ran up against fateful stiff opposition from almost all shades of power and opinion on the right-left political continuuum. The politically conservative were not placated by the work requirement, which in fact, was not really a work requirement, and those on the liberal-left opposed FAP for reasons of vested interests, according to Moynihan. The conservative response is not all that surprising, but the liberal-left response, which Moynihan attributed to naked self-interest, deserves some attention.

Whereas the politically conservative opposed FAP because it did not sufficiently insure that only "deserving" poor would benefit, those on the liberal-left declared their opposition to it ostensibly because it did not go far enough. They argued that $1,600 was insufficient—though FAP meant considerably more than $1,600, and they argued that the work requirement was oppressive—despite the fact that the work requirement in the liberal sponsored Work Incentive Program (WIN) of the Johnson Administration was considerably more oppressive. The real reason for much of the liberal-left opposition to FAP was, according to Moynihan, that it threatened the positions of the many middle class professionals employed in the social services fields. The results of all of the poverty strategies since the New Deal were, charges Moynihan, that the poor received numerous, and often ineffective, services, and, more importantly, the professionals got jobs and money:

> With astonishing consistency, middle class professionals—whatever their racial or ethnic backgrounds—when asked to devise ways of improving the condition of lower class groups, would come up with schemes of which the first effect would be to improve the condition of the middle class professionals, and the second effect might or might not be that of improving the condition of the poor. The programs of OEO were quintessentially of this kind. (1973, p. 54)

Until FAP, Moynihan charges, few recognized the essentially self-interest motivation of these middle class professionals, because, by and large, their self-interest and the interests of the poor were compatible. However, FAP changed all that and brought the interests into conflict. What ensued was but another manifestation of Gerhard E. Lenski's second postulate concerning the nature of man: "When men are confronted with important decisions where they are obliged to choose between their own or their group's interests and the interests of others, they nearly always choose the former—though often seeking to hide this fact from themselves and others" (1966, p. 30). Moynihan's narrative, as a case in point, is characteristically eloquent:

> the growth of welfare dependence and the initiation of federally financed welfare and anti-poverty activities under successive Democratic presidents had by the end of the 1960s created a large and strategically placed interest group. This interest group had to be affected by the Family Assistance proposal, and this in turn would be affected by the group's response. How would the heirs of the Webbs, "their allies in the higher ranks of the civil service, in the Left Wing of the labor movement, and among the Liberal intellecturals in the constituencies," respond? In a word, they did all in their power to insure that a guaranteed income was not enacted. (Moynihan, 1973, p. 306)

If the self-interest of many on the liberal-left was not sufficient to induce them to oppose FAP, there was another source of pressure which cajoled them into ignoring what Moynihan sees as the welfare of the poor. It is his view that the fate of FAP was sealed due to the unlucky timing circumstance of its being proposed at precisely the same time that the

National Welfare Rights Organization (NWRO) was emerging, and NWRO's leader opposed FAP. This opposition grew in intensity:

> When the president announced his FAP decision Wiley indicated that while he would at first be opposed, his opposition would be tactical, and that he would end up supporting the program. His August 6 letter to the president did not demand an immediate income guarantee at the $5,500 level but rather that "The Federal Government must take leadership in establishing *adequate income* for everyone as a national goal." He *could* have accepted the $2,400 level as a beginning. But this did not happen. NWRO opposition to FAP grew ever more determined until in the end it became obsessional.(Moynihan, 1973, p. 333)

According to Moynihan, the opposition of NWRO to FAP was solely the result of organizational interests, because FAP was correctly perceived of as primarily directed toward other poor than those of NWRO's constituency. The major beneficiaries of FAP would have been the working poor and Southern welfare families whereas NWRO was almost entirely made up of urban black welfare mothers. As NWRO opposition grew in intensity, so did its militant tactics.

> Even relatively strong, new organizations such as the Urban Coalition, and later Common Cause, had to proceed with care. The charismatic qualities of Wiley and the threatening tactics of his followers were a clear and present danger. For a white liberal to support FAP was to invite retaliation: speeches interrupted, meetings broken up, offices occupied, the epithet "racist" hurled with indifference. (Moynihan, 1973, p. 338)

In the end, FAP was defeated through what Moynihan characterizes as a coalition between ideological conservatives and the liberal-left. However, above and beyond Moynihan's animosity toward the liberal-left for what he sees as their selling out in order to protect their own interests, it remains highly doubtful whether FAP would have been able to overcome conservative opposition. The defeat might not have been as total had the liberal-left not sold out, but the original aims of FAP would probably not have been achieved since what might have emerged would have been a plan very different from the original one proposed. It has been seen that there has been strong resistance to the adoption of any guaranteed annual income because of the very strong belief in the need to protect the work incentive. There is a very prevalent deep fear that a guaranteed annual income would destroy the work incentive for those who are working, but whose earnings do not amount to much more than the guaranteed income. With all of its amendations, FAP never really overcame this fear.

Moreover, in terms of the argument of this work, there appears to be yet another problem with a guaranteed annual income which would render it self-defeating. Since the whole idea behind a guaranteed annual income is to provide a minimum "decent" subsistence level, and since there must always be provisions to protect the work incentive, would not that incentive have to be the desire to raise one's self above the minimum level, thereby making the minimum level indecent? We know, for example, that what is considered the poverty line today is considerably higher than what it was in the past; what is considered poverty in the United States might well be considered affluence in rural India. Poverty is *relative deprivation* (see Townsend, 1970, pp. 1-45, and Miller & Roby, pp. 124-145, in Townsend, 1970). This being the case, and as long as income is a function of employment and we believe and act on the premise that we must protect the work incentive, there can never be a minimum decent subsistence level. This does not mean that the whole notion of a guaranteed annual income is self-defeating. There are countries in Europe—Sweden, Denmark, and Holland, for example—where the guaranteed annual income does appear to operate successfully. Our criticism of the guaranteed annual income refers to its application in the United States with its deeply rooted individualistic ideology and work ethic. Where the work incentive must be so carefully guarded, the minimum subsistence level must, *ipso facto*, become indecent and undesirable, and as long as it remains indecent and undesirable, the non-poor will continue to stigmatize its undesirables, the poor, with the effects that have been analyzed.

A basic flaw in the strategies, proposals, and policies that have thus far been discussed is that they are designed to *assist the poor*; as such, they invariably contribute to the further isolation of the poor and enhance the stigma of poverty. So long as they remain "programs in aid of the poor," thus calling attention to the recipient's primary role and status as poor, these programs will continue to be seen as programs that burden the non-poor, that the non-poor are forced to *give* to the poor and for which the non-poor receive no return. This runs counter to what Alvin Gouldner (1960) has termed "The Norm of Reciprocity" (cf, Offenbacher, 1968), and is a basic fallacy in applying a limited conflict-theory approach. As long as the conflict limits, restricts, in accordance with the rules of the state, as long as those generating the conflict restrain themselves by precluding political revolution, then the non-poor retain the upper hand. Since they have vested interests in retaining their dominance, they have vested interests in maintaining and perpetuating poverty (cf. Gans, 1972), and this provides grounds for the non-poor's derivation of stigma-theories that rationalize their animosity for the poor—"parasites." This is especially likely to occur at times when the non-poor are experiencing economic difficulties. As has been shown, the poor are then especially singled out as the source of problems in the economy. Being so isolated, they are the most vulnerable, easily accessible scapegoats.

The conclusion to be drawn from our analysis, insofar as social policy is concerned, is that the most effective means of breaking the vicious circle, the stigma of poverty, is by creating and implementing policies and programs that will lead to the integration of the poor with the non-poor, rather than to their further isolation. We would not be so bold as to suggest that we have *the* answer as to how this integration is to be accomplished, for we are quite certain that there are no quick and easy answers; there are no panaceas. However, our analysis does suggest direction, and we will attempt to broadly outline a number of proposals toward that end.

It is somewhat revealing to observe that whereas in periods of economic strain, such as in the United States since 1971, the public clamors for tighter control of welfare funds, that same public is quite receptive to the extension of unemployment insurance benefits. This can be seen in the fact that in 1971 there was little opposition to the extension of the period covered by unemployment insurance in a number of states. There are, to be sure, a number of reasons for the difference in attitude toward welfare and unemployment insurance, such as the fact that unemployment insurance is precisely that—insurance—toward which the employer contributed while the employee was working, the fact that there is a time limit for receiving unemployment insurance, and the fact that unemployment insurance is for workers who want to work but have been laid off their jobs through no fault of their own. There is, we believe, yet another important reason for the difference in attitude toward unemployment insurance, which is that unemployment insurance is seen as a right to which any worker covered is entitled, whether he is a blue-collar worker, white-collar worker, or even a professional. The public is aware that even many engineers were laid off during the economic "crisis" and were sustained by unemployment insurance. It has been alleged, though we have no evidence to support the allegation, that it is not too uncommon for female employees to request their employers to fire them when they are about to leave their jobs to give birth. Whether or not this is a normal course of affairs, the point is that unemployment insurance carries with it little of the stigma attached to welfare because it is seen as a benefit that is distributed equally, in the sense that it is not a class-specific benefit. As such, it is a benefit with which the non-poor, as well as the poor, can identify.

The distinction between class-specific and class-transcending or universalistic benefits is crucial, because while it may be argued that welfare could be perceived in the same terms, that an originally non-poor individual might apply for welfare if he were to find himself destitute, the point is that as long as he is non-poor he does not visualize himself as being in the social category of a welfare recipient. The stigma and stigma theories that have been created over the centuries have resulted in a social category of poverty that is essentially different from that of the non-poor. As Goffman (1963b) puts it: "By definition, of course, we believe the person with a stigma is not quite human" (p. 6). The stigmatized poor, then, are a social category with which we cannot identify. They are categorically different from us (the non-poor).

Unemployment insurance, on the other hand, while we most certainly would not want to be forced into a position where we will have to make use of it, is not something that is reserved for a specific social category. Many people like ourselves have had to sustain themselves on it. Because it is class-transcendent rather than class-specific, unemployment insurance is an integrative, rather than an isolating, benefit. The non-poor individual can see something in it with which he can relate as a member of society, and thus he is not opposed to its extension.

A similar situation exists with reference to programs and policies for the aged. While it may very well be argued that the aged are a separate social category in and of themselves—and, indeed, a stigmatized one at that—its stigma is of a different nature than that of the poor; everyone, after all, who expects to survive anticipates being elderly. Thus, coupled with the conscience-placating and current responsibility-easing functions, our ability to more readily identify with the elderly makes us more receptive to policies and programs on their behalf.[24]

We would argue that effective social policies, integrating rather than isolating ones, would be those with which the non-poor as well as the poor can identify and in which they can see some benefit for themselves. As a first step, the move toward the integration of the poor must mean the end of all restrictions placed specifically on the lives of the poor. It is taken for granted in our society that the poor must be "regulated," and toward this end, anyone who wishes to receive welfare must be willing to accept certain restrictions on his behavior which are thereby entailed. But, as E. V. Walter (1970) has shown, this was not always the case:

> Hebrew methods of provisioning the poor included modes of distributing resources as well as modes of distributing products. Alms and tithes went along with the right to glean in fields, orchards, and vineyards. The fundamental principle in all the methods ensured that the poor were not excluded from resources and that they were not excluded from the community. (p. 29)

---

[24] This is not to suggest that our policies and programs for the aged are integrative. We simply wish to point out the willingness to spend monies on programs when the taxpayer sees in those programs a clear self-interest.

A number of measures have recently been taken, many as the result of court actions initiated by the National Welfare Rights Organization (NWRO), to insure that a welfare recipient's Constitutional and administrative rights are not abrogated. Along the same lines, a number of years ago, the New York City Department of Welfare (now called Department of Social Services) instituted on an experimental basis a plan in which a welfare applicant needed only to sign an affidavit of eligibility to be placed on the welfare rolls (there was spot-checking of the applications comparable to the extent of spot-checking of income tax returns), thereby reducing considerably the extensive and demeaning "investigative" process. It was reported at the time that this did not result in any appreciable increase in welfare expenditures. The Commissioner of Welfare, Mitchell I. Ginsberg, had justified this drastic step on the grounds that even if a number of unqualified applicants did receive money, this would be more than compensated for by the vast savings of that which the normal validation process would have cost. And, it was reported, the experiment proved to be a success both fiscally and administratively, which would seem to indicate that the only real "function" of the restrictions and means tests is to stigmatize and demoralize the applicant.

Means tests, at least in the suspecting and demeaning manner in which they are often administered, particularly to AFDC applicants, are an indication of the extent to which the recipient of aid is subject to stigmatization. The National Association of Social Workers has declared its "stand for the abolition of the means test in the archaic form in which it is applied." Harold Wilensky (1976) put it rather cogently when he argued that "we must abandon the worst legacy we inherited from Britain—an expensive, punitive machinery of means testing—and look closely at areas where the British and other Europeans excel (for example, in providing equitable, low-cost access to health services)" (p. 64). How ironic that Britain, from whom we inherited our means testing and which had a much longer tradition of stigmatizing the poor, should be so much more progressive in this area than is the United States.

It was stated in Chapter 4 that the stigma of poverty can be found to apply, with decreasing severity the farther removed one is from the core, to the entire lower class, and that receipt of assistance is the visibility factor which actualizes the stigmatization process. Evidence to support this contention is suggested by some of the findings of W. G. Runciman (1966) concerning the attitudes of manual and nonmanual workers in England toward state provision of various types of services. Assuming, as does Runciman on the basis of his data, that manual and nonmanual workers correspond to working class and middle class, it should come as no surprise that the middle class is much more reluctant to have the state provide services without means tests than is the working class (Runciman, 1966, pp. 223-226). The five provisions about which both classes were queried were: "family allowance for first child," "subsidized rent on house or flat," "free legal aid," "unemployment pay at full rate for as long as unemployed," and "free university education for all who can pass exams." On the question of free university education, the proportion who favored this provision without a means test was virtually identical for both classes (45%); on the other provisions, the percentages who favored no means test was lower for both classes. However, the proportion of those who did favor the other provisions without a means test was considerably higher for manual than for nonmanual workers. The breakdown for nonmanual workers was as follows:

Table 5.1 *Attitudes of non manual workers toward state provision of selected services*

	With means test	Without means test	Not at all
Family allowance for first child	31%	18%	48%
Subsidized rent on house or flat	47	7	40
Free legal aid	67	19	9
Unemployment pay at full rate for as long as unemployed	46	15	30
Free university education for all who can pass exams	45	45	7

Source: Adapted from W. G. Runciman, *Relative Deprivation and Social Justice*, Berkeley; University of California Press, 1966, p. 225, Table 30.

The strong opposition of nonmanual workers (middle class) to family allowance for first child and unemployment pay at full rate for as long as unemployed may be rooted in the middle class stigma of poverty which defines those below them, even persons in the working class, as of suspect sexual morality—"if you offer them a family allowance they'll breed like rabbits"—and as lazy.

Runciman (1966) interprets the favorable middle class attitude toward free university education as being rooted in their self-interest:

> Middle class parents have come to feel the need for state provision in a matter which was traditionally confined to middle class families and for which they themselves expected to have to pay. What they feel as the decline in their relative economic condition, therefore, has not only led them to feel a greater need for state

> assistance for something which they can less afford: it has also led them to feel that if state provision is being made for families which in the past seldom sent a child to university at all, then they are entitled to benefit from this provision also. (pp. 225-226)

If there is a similar middle class psychology in America, this finding lends support to our argument for class-transcending benefits.

As a second preliminary step, a massive educational venture for the non-poor as to the nature of the composition of the welfare caseloads might be somewhat effective in, at least, easing the stigma. Projects of this nature have recently been undertaken by various groups, such as the Social and Rehabilitation Service of the U.S. Department of Health, Education and Welfare (see their pamphlet, "Welfare Myths Versus Fact," 1971), The League of Women Voters, numerous coalitions for welfare reform, etc., but so far they seem to have had little effect if for no other reason than that the mass media persist in presenting singular instances of irregularities (due, not infrequently to administrative error rather than to client deceit) and fraud as if they were the norm.

Neither of these two preliminary steps, however, can accomplish anything more than a softening of the stigma, making it easier to live with. They cannot really accomplish the integration of the poor. What they might accomplish is to bring more of the poor a bit closer, to induce many of the poor who do not now avail themselves of welfare to partake in its services. But, in and of themselves, they cannot effect any basic change, and whatever softening of the stigma might occur would undoubtedly be only temporary, because the increased welfare budgets which would be required would cause a reversion back to the rigid stigma of poverty. This should have been the lesson of the 1960s in America, which began on a very idealistic note and ended with a distinct harshening of the stigma of poverty.

To effect basic change in the stigma of poverty, to really integrate the poor, requires, as we have suggested, the designing and implementation of policies and programs in which the non-poor can see clear benefits for themselves and with which they can themselves identify. This means the creation of programs that are designed for the benefit of all in the society, as a right of citizenship, if you will, and not because of membership in a particular class (the lower class) which experiences economic "problems." This means the availability and extension of services to all, as members of the society, rather than as members of a particular segment of the society. Along these lines, Alfred J. Kahn and Sheila B. Kamerman (1975) have recently argued that in the United States we must cease thinking of social services and public welfare as being limited solely to the poor and troubled. Rather, we must recognize that there are essentially only two categories, "social services and benefits connected to problems and breakdowns (and *these* are not limited to the poor), and *social services and benefits needed by average people under ordinary circumstances*" (p. x, emphasis in original). After surveying a variety of European social services, they suggest that we carefully develop an adequate system of "*public social utilities*" (p. 172) which, like other public utilities, are available to all in the society. It is not only the poor who have needs and problems, and the United States should, therefore, emphasize the need of "social services for all" (pp. 171ff). We would add that by doing so, not only would the needs of a much broader segment of the population be addressed but, simultaneously, there would be services available that would serve to integrate, in place of those that currently isolate, the poor.

Richard M. Titmuss has been one of the strongest proponents of the universalizing of social services. He cites the British post-war National Service Act, Education Act of 1944, National Insurance Act, and Family Allowance Act as embodying the principle of universalism:

> One fundamental historical reason for the adoption of this principle was the aim of making services available and accessible to the whole population in such ways as would not involve users in any humiliating loss of status, dignity or self respect. There should be no sense of inferiority, pauperism, shame or stigma in the use of a publicly provided service; no attribution that one was being or becoming a "public burden." Hence the emphasis on the social rights of all citizens to use or not to use as responsible people the services made available by the community in respect of certain needs which the private market and the family were unable or unwilling to provide universally. If these services were not provided for everybody by everybody they would either not be available at all, or only to those who could afford them, and for others on such terms as would involve the infliction of a sense of inferiority and stigma. (1968, p. 129)

If England has found difficulties in realizing and actualizing universalistic social services, the problems facing such an attempt in American society are even more complicated by its strong ideology of individualism (cf. Lipset, 1970, pp. 51-53), and by the lack or coordination between the federal, state, and local governments and agencies involved with the dispensing of social services. As S. M. Miller and Pamela A. Roby (1970a) have pointed out:

> Since 1937...the number of private as well as public, local, regional, and federal organizations governing the affairs of the American people has multiplied. The resulting structure of government—multileveled, overlapping, peculiarly dispersed—is clearly a major problem of American society. In addition to the problems of government coordination that have been inherited from the past, structural incoherencies arise as a result of the rapid expansion of communities and as a consequence of the powerful defenders of laissez faire who effectively shun coordinated governmental efforts. (pp. 229-230)

Difficult as it may be to achieve the broadening of services aspired to by Miller and Roby, the realization of Titmuss' ultimate objective is open to even more doubt, for to Titmuss universal social service is only the first step in a two-step process, the second step being positive discrimination to overcome social inequality. Titmuss (1968) defines it as a challenge:

> The challenge that faces us is not the choice between universalist and selective social services. The real challenge resides in the question: what particular infrastructure of universalist services is needed in order to provide a framework of values and opportunity bases within and around which can be developed socially acceptable selective services aiming to discriminate positively, with the minimum risk of stigma, in favor of those whose needs are greatest. (p. 135)

His argument for positive discrimination derives from his keen sensitivity to the effects of the stigma of poverty upon the poor and his conviction that our poverty policies up to now have not fully appreciated those effects:

> We overestimated the potentialities of the poor, without help, to understand and manipulate an increasingly *ad hoc* society, and we failed to understand the indignities of expecting the poor to identify themselves as poor people and to declare, in effect, "I am an unequal person" (p. 163)

If the American experience with "affirmative action" is any indication, the prospects for introducing universalistic, positively discriminatory social services do not appear to be very bright. The furor surrounding the case of ***DeFunis v Odegaard*** (United States Supreme Court, 1974)[25]

[25]*DeFunis v. Odegaard,* 82 Wash. 2d 11, 507 P. 2d 1169, (1974); *Vacated as Moot,*–U.S.–, S. Ct., No. 73-235, April 23, 1974.

indicates that positive discrimination may run into stiff opposition even by many on the liberal-left.

On the other hand, perhaps because Titmuss' notion of positive discrimination would be class-based, rather than being racially or ethnically based, its chances for adoption may be somewhat higher. This very distinction between class-based and ethnically based discrimination was alluded to by former Supreme Court Justice William O. Douglas in his dissenting opinion in the case of *De Funis v. Odegaard*, when he argued that, "[t]he key to the problem is the consideration of each application *in a racially neutral way*."[26] Douglas indicated his sympathy with a policy that would give special consideration to those with "prior handicaps," but,

> Such a policy would not be limited to Blacks, or Chicanos or Filipinos or American Indians, although undoubtedly groups such as these may in practice be the principal beneficiaries of it. But a poor Appalachian white, or a second generation Chinese in San Francisco, or some other American whose lineage is so diverse as to defy ethnic labels, may demonstrate similar potential and thus be accorded favorable consideration by the committee. (pp. 12-13)

However, if past decisions of the Supreme Court are any indication, as they almost certainly are, not only can we rule out the possibility of positive class-based discrimination, discrimination in favor of the poor, but it even seems highly doubtful that the Court will strike down those practices that have for so long discriminated against the poor (cf. Michelman, 1969).

Elementary as the proposal for class-transcendent social policy appears, it opens up a "pandora's box," and perhaps raises many more questions than it answers. First of all, it assumes that the aim of social policy is to actually *solve* the problem, in this case to integrate the poor, rather than to *control* the effects of the problem, to "keep the poor in their place." It presents an image of objective social policy and policy makers, rather than emphasizing the conflicting self-interests between competing factions within the society. It, thus, ignores the whole question of from where the resources to pay for these programs and services will come. It is not quite adequate to say that, of course, all this will entail a major redistribution of resources. The recent experiences in Sweden indicate that even with a strong idealism, the burden of paying for services can become so overbearing as to cause "the welfare state [to go] crazy" (Gunnar Myrdal, quoted in *New York Times,* 1971).

---

[26] –U.S.–, (S. Ct., No. 73-235, April 23, 1974, p. 15.) *dissenting opinion*. Emphasis in original.

Despite the heavy tax burden which resulted in massive strikes by middle class professionals, poverty persists in Sweden both within and between generations. The overall assistance rates between 1945 and 1973 fluctuated between 6.2 to 6.4 to 6.0 percent of the population (Korpi, 1976, p. 128). While the proportion of older people receiving assistance decreased, "the proportion of persons in the ages 16-39 has strongly increased" (p. 131). Moreover, despite the "efforts by the authorities to establish social assistance as a citizen's right, the stigma which by tradition is attached to 'welfare clients' still remains strong in Sweden" (p. 121).

The extent to which the high taxes required to support Sweden's social services were a major factor in the defeat of Olof Palme's Social Democratic Party in September 1976, remains to be determined. Whereas initial reports indicated that high taxes were a major campaign issue (Weinraub, 1976, p. 1) others have suggested that the real issue was an unrelated environmental one. Several months before the elections, Harold Wilensky (1976) averred that the "revolt of the middle mass in the world's most celebrated welfare state has been contained, partly through diversified financing and a fair net income" (p. 16). Whether Wilensky's assessment is accurate will be indicated by the policies of the new government. In any case, it is clear that complex economic and ideological issues are involved.

In the final analysis, the question of whether this integration can be achieved relates to one of the basic theoretical questions in the area of social stratification—the "function" or "dysfunction" and inevitability of inequality (see debate between K. Davis—W. Moore and M. M. Tumin, reprinted in Tumin, 1970), and we are not yet in any position to determine whether it is or is not feasible (we have, thus far, "determined" it to be nonexistent, but this does not mean that it is a theoretical impossibility). That we may never be able to accomplish ultimate integration and equality remains a distinct possibility. To assume that we shall ever solve the problem completely is, quite possibly, a delusion, if for no other reason than that the very "solution" of one problem creates new ones.

The above analysis led us to see the persistence of poverty and the patterns of behavior and attitudes of the poor as a "dependent subculture," which is in turn self-perpetuating. That is, it is internalized and transmitted through socialization, but it is also *dependent* upon the nonpoor, specifically, the stigma of poverty. It is, thus, both subcultural and situational, simultaneously. As Hans Gerth and C. Wright Mills (1953) put it:

> if the upper classes monopolize the means of communication and fill the several mass media with the idea that all those at the bottom are there because they are lazy, unintelligent, and in gen-

> eral inferior, then these appraisals may be taken over by the poor and used in the building of an image of their selves. The appraisal of the wealthy, privileged children may then be internalized by underprivileged children and facilitate negative self-images. Such images, if impressed early enough by all persons who are significant to these children may cripple their chances to better their social position and thus obtain economic and social bases for more favorable self-images. (pp. 88-89)

We would emphasize that the "significant others" of which they speak include both the poor themselves and the non-poor.

The approach taken during the 1960s to break the "reign of error" of the stigma of poverty proved to be unsuccessful because, as Kenneth Clark pointed out (Clark & Hopkins, 1970), it failed to recognize the extent to which the stigma has been internalized, so as to make the poor unable to affect effective change.

We conclude, on the other hand, that to break the stigma of poverty the poor must be integrated, rather than isolated, and we suggest that steps in that direction must involve the creation and expansion of services and income maintenance that are available to all members of the society, thus affording the non-poor a basis for identifying with and seeing self-interest in these changes. The extent to which this can be accomplished remains in doubt; quite possibly there will never be complete integration. But along that path, services will be made available to both the poor and the non-poor, and they will, perhaps, reduce the isolation.

As was stated earlier, in contrast with Moynihan, the evaluation of social policy, by definition, must be based upon some standard which implies the formulation of social policy. The conclusion derived from the foregoing analysis points to the requirement for integrating, rather than the heretofore isolating, social policies. Toward this end, then, from the conclusions of this analysis emerges an operational index for the evaluation of social policy. Specifically, whatever the short-range benefits, the basic question must be: Will the program and policy, in the long run, lead to the integration of the poor into the society, or will it inevitably lead to their further isolation? The lesson of the 1960s should clearly be that short-run benefits can be very self-defeating in terms of this long-range objective—namely, the integration of the poor and the dissipation of the stigma of poverty.

BIBLIOGRAPHY

Alston, Jon P., & Dean, K. Imogene. "Socioeconomic Factors Associated with Attitudes Toward Welfare Recipients and the Causes of Poverty." *The Social Service Review,* 1972, Vol. 46, No. 1, pp. 13-23.

Altshuler, Alan A. *Community Control.* New York: Pegasus, 1970.

Anderson, Charles H. *Toward a New Sociology: A Critical View.* Homewood, Ill.: The Dorsey Press, 1971.

Banfield, Edward C. *The Unheavenly City.* Boston: Little, Brown, 1970.

Bell, Daniel. *The End of Ideology.* Revised Edition, New York: The Free Press, 1962.

Bendix, Rheinhard, & Lipset, Seymour Martin (Eds.). *Class, Status and Power.* Glencoe: The Free Press, 1953, Second Edition, 1966.

Bereiter, Carl. "A Non-psychological Approach to Early Compensatory Education." In Martin Deutch, Irwin Katz, & Arthur R. Jensen (Eds.), *Social Class, Race, and Psychological Development.* New York: Holt, Rinehart & Winston, 1968 . Pp. 337-346.

Berger, Peter L. *Invitation to Sociology.* Garden City: Doubleday Anchor Books, 1963.

Berger, Peter L. *The Sacred Canopy.* Garden City: Doubleday, 1967.

Berger, Peter L., & Luckmann, Thomas. *The Social Construction of Reality.* Garden City: Doubleday, 1966.

Bernstein, Basil. "Social Class and Linguistic Development: A Theory of Social Learning." In A. H. Halsey, J. Floud, & C. A. Anderson (Eds.) *Education, Economy and Society.* New York: The Free Press of Glencoe, 1962. Pp. 288-314.

Bernstein, Basil. "Social Class, Speech Systems, and Psychotherapy." In Frank Riessman, Jerome Cohen, & Arthur Pearl (Eds), *Mental Health of the Poor.* New York: The Free Press, 1964. Pp. 194-204.

Bernstein, Basil. "Linguistic Codes, Hesitation Phenomena and Intelligence." In Everett T. Keach, Jr., Robert Fulton, & William E. Gardner (Eds.), *Education and Social Crisis.* New York: Wiley, 1967. Pp. 179-192.

Bernstein, Basil B. "A Critique of the Concept 'Compensatory Education.' " In D. Wedderburn (Ed.), *Poverty, Inequality and Class Structure.* London: Cambridge University Press, 1974. Pp. 109-122.

Berube, Maurice R., & Gittell, Marilyn (Eds.). *Confrontation at Ocean Hill-Brownsville.* New York: Praeger, 1969.

Birnbaum, Norman. "Conflicting Interpretations of the Rise Of Capitalism: Marx and Weber." *British Journal of Sociology,* June 1953, Vol. IV, pp. 125-141.

Booth, Charles. *Life and Labour of the People in London.* 17 vols. London: Macmillan, 1902-3.

Booth, Charles. *Poor Law Reform.* London: Macmillan, 1910.

Bronfenbrenner, Urie. "Socialization and Social Class Through Time and Space." In Eleanor E. Maccoby, Theodore H. Newcomb, & Eugene L. Hartley (Eds.), *Readings in Social Psychology,* Third Edition. New York: Holt, Rinehart & Winston, 1958. Pp. 400-425.

Calhoun, John B. "Population Density and Social Pathology." In Leonard J. Duhl (Ed.), *The Urban Condition.* New York. Basic Books, 1963. Pp. 33-43.

Carter, Charles H. (Ed.). *Medical Aspects of Mental Retardation.* Springfield, Ill.: Thomas, 1965.

Chinoy, Ely. *Automobile Workers and the American Dream.* Garden City: Doubleday, 1955.

Clark, John P., & Wenninger, Eugene P. "Socio-Economic Class and Area as Correlates of Illegal Behavior Among Juveniles." *American Sociological Review,* 1962, Vol. 27, No. 6, pp. 826-834.

Clark, Kenneth B. *Dark Ghetto.* New York: Harper Torchbooks, 1967.

Clark, Kenneth B., & Hopkins, Jeannette. *A Relevant War Against Poverty.* New York: Harper Torchbooks, 1970.

Clausen, John A., & Kohn, Melvin. "Relation of Schizophrenia to the Social Structure of a Small City." In Benjamin Pasamanick (Ed.), *Epidemiology of Mental Disorder.* Washington, D. C.: American Association for the Advancement of Science, 1959. Pp. 69-86.

Cloward, Richard A. "A Strategy of Disruption." Tape recording of a paper delivered at the Center for the Study of Democratic Institutions, Santa Barbara, California, 1966.

Cloward, Richard A., & Elman, Richard M. "Poverty, Injustice and the Welfare State." *The Nation,* Feb. 28, 1966 and March 7, 1966.

Cloward, Richard A., & Ohlin, Lloyd E. *Delinquency and Opportunity.* New York: The Free Press, 1960.

Cloward, Richard A., & Piven, Frances Fox. "The Weight of the Poor: A Strategy to End Poverty." In Chaim I. Waxman (Ed.), *Poverty: Power and Politics.* New York: Grosset & Dunlap, 1968. Pp. 311-327.

Cohen, Albert K. *Delinquent Boys.* New York: The Free Press, 1955.

Cohen, Albert K., & Short, James F., Jr. "Research in Delinquent Subcultures." *Journal of Social Issues,* 1958, Vol. XIV, pp. 20-37.

Cooley, Charles Horton. *Social Organization.* Introduction by Philip Rieff. New York: Schocken Books, 1962.

Cooley, Charles Horton, *Human Nature and the Social Order*. Introduction by Philip Rieff. New York: Schocken Books, 1964.

Coser, Lewis A. "Unanticipated Conservative Consequences of Liberal Theorizing." *Social Problems,* 1968-69, Vol. 16, pp. 263-272.

Cressey, Donald R. "Crime," In Robert K. Merton, & Robert A. Nisbet (Eds.), *Contemporary Social Problems,* Second Edition. New York: Harcourt, Brace & World, 1966. Pp. 136-192.

Cressey, Donald R. *Theft of the Nation.* New York: Harper Colophon Books, 1969.

Cressey, Donald R. *Other People's Money.* Belmont, Calif.: Wadsworth, 1970.

Culley, William J. "Nutrition and Mental Retardation." In Charles H. Carter (Ed.), *Medical Aspects of Mental Retardation.* Springfield, Ill.: Thomas, 1965.

Davis, Allison. *Social-Class Influences Upon Learning.* Cambridge: Harvard University Press, 1948.

Davis, Allison, & Dollard, John. *Children of Bondage.* New York: Harper Torchbooks, 1964.

Defoe, Daniel. *Giving Alms No Charity, and Employing the Poor a Grievance to the Nation,* 1704.

Dentler, Robert A. "A Critique of Education Projects in Community Action Programs." In Robert A. Dentler, Bernard Mackler, & Mary Ellen Warshauer (Eds.), *The Urban R's.* New York: Praeger, 1967. Pp. 158-174.

de Schweinitz, Karl. *England's Road to Social Security.* New York: Barnes, 1961.

Deutch, Martin P. "The Disadvantaged Child and the Learning Process." In Frank Riessman, Jerome Cohen, & Arthur Pearl (Eds.) *Mental Health of the Poor.* New York: The Free Press, 1964. Pp. 172-187.

Deutch, Martin P., Katz, Irwin & Jensen, Arthur (Eds.), *Social Class, Race, and Psychological Development.* New York: Holt, Rinehart & Winston, 1968.

Dollard, John. *Caste and Class in a Southern Town.* Garden City: Doubleday Anchor Books, 1957.

Donovan, John C. *The Politics of Poverty.* New York: Pegasus, 1967.

Duhl, Leonard J. (Ed.). *The Urban Condition.* New York: Basic Books, 1963.

Dunham, H. Warren, *Community and Schizophrenia: An Epidemiological Analysis.* Detroit: Wayne State University Press, 1965.

Dunham, H. Warren, Phillips, Patricia, & Srinivasan, Barbara. "A Research Note on Diagnosed Mental Illness and Social Class." *American Sociological Review,* 1966, Vol. 31, pp. 223-227.

Edwards, G. Franklin (Ed.). *E. Franklin Frazier on Race Relations.* Chicago: University of Chicago Press, 1968.

Elman, Richard M. *The Poorhouse State.* New York: Pantheon, 1965.
Essien-Udom, E. U. *Black Nationalism.* Chicago: University of Chicago Press, 1962.
Faris, Robert E. L., & Dunham, H. Warren. *Mental Disorders in Urban Areas.* Chicago: University of Chicago Press, 1939.
Feagin, Joe R. *Subordinating the Poor.*Englewood Cliffs: Prentice Hall, 1975.
Ferman, Louis A., Kormbluh, Joyce L., Haber, Alan. *Poverty in America.* Revised Edition. Ann Arbor: University of Michigan Press, 1968.
Feuer, Lewis S. (Ed.). *Marx and Engels: Basic Writings on Politics and Philosophy.* New York: Doubleday Anchor Books, 1959.
Finestone, Harold. "Cats, Kicks and Color." *Social Problems,* 1957, Vol. 5, pp. 3-13.
Finney, Joseph C. (Ed.). *Culture Change, Mental Health, and Poverty.* New York: Clarion Books, 1970.
Frazier, E. Franklin. *The Negro Family in the United States,* 1939. Revised and Abridged with a New Foreword by Nathan Glazer. Chicago: University of Chicago Press, 1966.
Frazier, E. Franklin. *Negro Youth at the Crossways.* New York: Schocken Books, 1967.
Frazier, E. Franklin. "Theoretical Structure of Sociology and Sociological Research." In G. Franklin Edwards (Ed.), *E. Franklin Frazier on Race Relations.* Chicago: University of Chicago Press, 1968. Pp. 3-29.
Free, Lloyd, A., & Cantril, Hadley. *The Political Beliefs of Americans: A Study of Public Opinion.* New Brunswick, N.J.: Rutgers University Press, 1967.
Freedman, Jonathan L. *Crowding and Behavior.* San Francisco: Freeman, 1975.
Friedman, Rose E. *Poverty: Definition and Perspective.* Washington, D. C.: American Enterprise Institute for Public Policy Research, 1965.
Fuchs, Estelle. *Pickets at the Gate.* New York: The Free Press, 1966.
Galbraith, John Kenneth. *The Affluent Society.* Boston: Houghton Mifflin, 1958.
Gans, Herbert J. *The Urban Villagers.* New York: The Free Press, 1962.
Gans, Herbert J. "Poverty and Culture: Some Basic Questions About Studying Life-Styles of the Poor." In Peter Townsend (Ed.), *The Concept of Poverty.* New York: American Elsevier, 1970. Pp. 146-164.
Gans, Herbert J. "The Positive Functions of Poverty." *American Journal of Sociology,* 1972, Vol. 78, No. 2, pp. 275-289.
Gerth, Hans, & Mills, C. Wright. *Character and Social Structure.* New York: Harcourt, Brace & World, 1953.
Gittell, Marilyn, & Hevesi, Alan G. *The Politics of Urban Education.* New York: Praeger, 1969.

Glaser, Daniel (Ed.). *Handbook of Criminology.* Chicago: Rand McNally, 1974.

Glazer, Nathan. "The Grand Design of the Poverty Program." In Chaim I. Waxman (Ed.), *Poverty: Power and Politics.* New York: Grosset & Dunlap, 1968. Pp. 281-292.

Goffman, Erving. *Behavior in Public Places.* New York: The Free Press, 1963a.

Goffman, Erving. *Stigma: Notes on the Management of Spoiled Identity.* Englewood Cliffs, N.J.: Prentice Hall, 1963b.

Gordon, Milton M. "The Concept of Sub-Culture and Its Application." *Social Forces,* 1947, Vol. 26, pp. 40-42 .

Gouldner, Alvin W. "The Norm of Reciprocity." *American Sociological Review,* Vol. 25, 1960, pp. 161-178.

Gouldner, Alvin W., & Miller, S.M. (Eds.). *Applied Sociology.* New York: The Free Press, 1965.

Gouldner, Alvin W. "The Sociologist as Partisan: Sociology and the Welfare State." *The American Sociologist,* 1968, Vol. 3, pp. 103-116.

Gouldner, Alvin W. "Toward the Radical Reconstruction of Sociology." *Social Policy,* May/June 1970, pp. 18-25.

Gove, Walter R. "Societal Reaction as an Explanation of Mental Illness: An Evaluation." *American Sociological Review,* October 1970, Vol. 35, No. 5, pp. 873-884.

Green, Arnold W. "The Middle Class Child and Neurosis." *American Sociological Review,* 1946, Vol. 11, No. 1, pp. 31-41.

Green, Arnold W. *Social Problems: Arena of Conflict.* New York: McGraw-Hill, 1975.

Haggstrom, Warren C. "The Power of the Poor." In Chaim I. Waxman, (Ed.), *Poverty: Power and Politics.* New York: Grosset & Dunlap, 1968. Pp. 113-136.

Han, Wan Sang. "Two Conflicting Themes: Common Values Versus Class Differential Values." *American Sociological Review,* 1969, Vol. 24, pp. 679-690.

Handel, Gerald, & Rainwater, Lee. "Working Class People and Family Planning." *Social Work,* 1961, Vol. 6, pp. 18-25.

Harrington, Michael. *The Other America.* New York: Macmillan, 1962.

Harris, Marvin. *The Nature of Cultural Things.* New York: Random House, 1964.

Havighurst, Robert J. "Social Class and Color Differences in Child Rearing." *American Sociological Review,* 1946, Vol. 11, pp. 698-710.

Heilbroner, Robert. *The Worldly Philosophers.* Third Edition. New York: Clarion Books, 1967.

Herskovits, Melville J. *Man and His Works.* New York: Knopf, 1948.

Hirschi, Travis. *Causes of Delinquency.* Berkeley: University of California Press, 1969.

Hoffer, Abram. *Niacin Therapy in Psychiatry.* Springfield, Ill.: Thomas, 1962.

Hollingshead, August B. *Elmtown's Youth.* New York: Wiley Science Editions, 1961.

Hollingshead, August B., & Redlich, F. C. *Social Class and Mental Illness.* New York: Wiley, 1958.

Hollingshead, August B., & Rogler, L. H. "Attitudes Toward Slums and Public Housing in Puerto Rico." In Leonard J. Duhl, (Ed.), *The Urban Condition.* New York: Basic Books, 1963. Pp. 229-245.

Honigmann, John J. "Psychiatry and the Culture of Poverty." *Kansas Journal of Sociology,* 1965, Vol. 1, pp. 162-165.

Honigmann, John J. "Middle Class Values and Cross-Cultural Understanding." In Joseph C. Finney, (Ed.), *Culture Change, Mental Health, and Poverty.* New York: Clarion Books, 1970. Pp. 1-19.

Horowitz, Irving Louis. *Professing Sociology.* Chicago: Aldine, 1968.

Hunt, J. McVicker. *The Challenge of Incompetence and Poverty: Papers on the Role of Early Education.* Urbana: University of Illinois Press. 1969.

Hunter, Robert. *Poverty: Social Conscience in the Progressive Era,* 1904. Reprinted with an Introduction and Notes by Peter d'A Jones. New York: Harper Torchbooks, 1965.

Hurley, Rodger. *Poverty and Mental Retardation:* A Causal Relationship. New York: Random House, 1969.

Hyman, Herbert H. "The Value Systems of Different Classes." In Reinhard Bendix & Seymour Martin Lipset (Eds.), *Class, Status and Power.* Glencoe: The Free Press, 1953, 1953. Pp. 426-442.

Jaffe, Frederick, & Polgar, Steven. "Family Planning and Public Policy: Is the 'Culture of Poverty' the New Cop-Out?" *Journal of Marriage and the Family,* 1968, Vol. 30, pp. 228-235.

Janowitz, Morris (Ed.). *W. I. Thomas on Social Organization and Social Personality.* Chicago: University of Chicago Press, 1966.

John, Vera P. "The Intellectual Development of Slum Children: Some Preliminary Findings." *American Journal of Orthopsychiatry,* 1963, Vol. XXXIII, pp. 813-822.

John, Vera P. "The Basil Bernstein Fad." Paper presented at the Annual Meeting of the American Anthropological Association, November 1966, mimeographed.

John, Vera P., & Goldstein, L. S. "The Social Context of Language Acquisition." *Merrill Palmer Quarterly,* 1964, Vol. 10, pp. 265-275.

Johnson, Charles S. *Growing Up in the Black Belt.* New York: Schocken Books, 1967.

Jordan, W. K. *Philanthropy in England, 1480-1660.* New York: Russell Sage Foundation, 1959.

Kahl, Joseph A. *The American Class Structure.* New York: Holt, Rinehart & Winston, 1957.

Kahn, Alfred J., & Kamerman, Sheila B. *Not for the Poor Alone.* Philadelphia: Temple University Press, 1975.

Kallen, David J., & Miller, Dorothy. "Public Attitudes Toward Welfare." *Social Work,* July 1971, Vol. 16, No. 3, pp. 83-90.

Kluckhohn, Clyde. *Culture and Behavior.* New York: The Free Press, 1962.

Kohn, Melvin L. "Social Class and the Exercise of Parental Authority." *American Sociological Review,* 1959, Vol. 24, pp. 352-366.

Korpi, Walter. "Poverty, Social Policy in Sweden, 1945-72." In Richard Scase (Ed.), *Readings in the Swedish Class Structure.* Oxford and New York: Pergamon Press, 1976. Pp. 119-149.

Kriesberg, Louis. *Mothers in Poverty.* Chicago: Aldine, 1970.

Kroeber, Alfred L. *Anthropology.* Revised Edition. New York: Harcourt, Brace & World, 1948.

Kroeber, Alfred L. & Kluckhohn, Clyde. *Culture.* New York: Vintage Books, 1952.

Krosney, Herbert. *Beyond Welfare: Poverty in the Supercity.* New York: Holt, Rinehart & Winston, 1966.

Lander, Bernard, & Lander, Nathan. "Deprivation as a Cause of Delinquency: Economic or Moral?" In Bernard Rosenberg, Israel Gerver, & F. William Howton (Eds.), *Mass Society in Crisis.* New York: Macmillan, 1964. Pp. 130-141.

Langner, Thomas S. *Life Stress and Mental Health.* New York: The Free Press, 1963.

Leacock, Eleanor. "Distortions of Working-Class Reality in American Social Science." *Science and Society,* 1967, Vol. XXXI, pp. 1-20.

Lenski, Gerhard. *Power and Privilege.* New York: McGraw-Hill, 1966.

Levin, H. M. (Ed.). *Community Control of Schools.* New York: Clarion Books, 1970.

Levitan, Sar A. *The Great Society's Poor Law.* Baltimore: Johns Hopkins University Press, 1969.

Lewis, Hylan. "Child Rearing Practices Among Low Income Families in the District of Columbia, Washington, D. C." *Cross-Tell,* February 1967.

Lewis, Hylan. "Culture, Class and Family Life Among Low-Income Urban Negroes." In Arthur M. Ross & Herbert Hill (Eds.), *Employment, Race and Poverty.* New York: Harcourt, Brace & World, 1967b. Pp. 149-172.

Lewis, Oscar. *Five Families.* New York: Basic Books, 1959.

Lewis, Oscar. *The Children of Sanchez.* New York: Random House, 1961.

Lewis, Oscar. "The Culture of Poverty." *Trans-Action,* November 1963, pp. 17-19.

Lewis, Oscar. *La Vida.* New York: Random House, 1966.
Lewis, Oscar. "The Children of Sanchez, Pedro Martinez, and La Vida: A CA Book Review," *Current Anthropology,* 1967, Vol. 8, pp. 480-500.
Lewis, Oscar. *A Study of Slum Culture.* New York: Random House, 1968.
Lewis, Oscar. Review of Charles A. Valentine. "Culture and Poverty." *Caribbean Review,* Spring 1969, Vol. 1, No. 1, pp. 5-6.
Lewis, Oscar, "The Culture of Poverty." *Scientific American,* October 1966, Vol. 215, No. 4, pp. 19-25.
Lewis, Oscar. "A Puerto Rican Boy." In Joseph C. Finney (Ed.), *Culture Change, Mental Health, and Poverty.* New York: Clarion Books, 1970. Pp. 149-154.
Liebow, Elliot. *Talley's Corner.* Boston: Little, Brown, 1967.
Lincoln, C. Eric. *The Black Muslims in America.* Boston: Beacon Press, 1961.
Linton, Ralph. *The Study of Man.* New York: Appleton-Century, 1936.
Lipset, Seymour Martin. *Revolution and Counterrevolution.* Revised Edition. Garden City: Doubleday Anchor Books, 1970.
Loch, Charles S. *Charity Organisation.* Second Edition. London: Swan Sonnenschein, 1892.
Maccoby, Eleanor, Newcomb, Theodore H., Hartley, Eugene L. (Eds.). *Readings in Social Psychology.* New York: Holt, Rinehart & Winston, 1958.
Malthus, Thomas Robert. *Essay on the Principle of Population.* Baltimore: Penguin Books, 1971.
Mannhein, Karl. *Ideology and Utopia.* London: Routledge and Kegan Paul, 1936.
Marris, Peter, & Rein, Martin. *Dilemmas of Social Reform.* New York: Atherton Press, 1967.
Marshall, T. H. *Social Policy.* London: Hutchinson University Press, 1965.
Marx, Karl. *The Eighteenth Brumaire of Louis Bonaparte.* New York: International Publishers, 1963.
Matza, David. *Delinquency and Drift.* New York: Wiley, 1964.
Matza, David. "The Disreputable Poor." In Rheinhard Bendix & Seymour Martin Lipset (Eds.), *Class, Status, and Power.* Second Edition. New York: The Free Press, 1966a. Pp. 289-302.
Matza, David. "Poverty and Disrepute." In Robert K. Merton, and Robert A. Nisbet (Eds.), *Contemporary Social Problems,* Second Edition. New York: Harcourt, Brace and World, 1966b. Pp. 619-669.
Mayer, Kurt B., & Buckley, Walter. *Class and Society.* Third Edition. New York: Random House, 1970.
Mayer, Martin. *Teachers' Strike: New York, 1968.* New York: Harper & Row, 1969.

Merton, Robert K. "Social Structure and Anomie." *American Sociological Review,* 1938, Vol. 3, pp. 672-682.

Merton, Robert R. *Social Theory and Social Structure,* Enlarged Edition. New York: The Free Press, 1968.

Merton, Robert K., & Nisbet, Robert A. (Eds.) *Contemporary Social Problems,* Second Edition. New York: Harcourt, Brace and World, 1966.

Michelman, Frank I. "On Protecting the Poor Through the Fourteenth Amendment." *Harvard Law Review,* November 1969, Vol. 83, No. 1, pp. 7-59.

Miller, S. M. "The American Lower Classes: A Typological Approach." *Social Research,* 1964, Vol. 31, No. 1, pp. 1-22.

Miller, S. M., & Mishler, Elliott G. "Social Class, Mental Illness, and American Psychiatry: An Expository Review." In Frank Riessman, Jerome Cohen, & Arthur Pearl, (Eds.), *Mental Health of the Poor.* New York: The Free Press, 1964. Pp. 16-36.

Miller, S. M., & Roby, Pamela. "Poverty: Changing Social Stratification." In Peter Townsend (Ed.), *The Concept of Poverty.* New York: American Elsevier, 1970. Pp. 124-145.

Miller, S. M., & Roby, Pamela. *The Future of Inequality.* New York: Basic Books, 1970a.

Miller, S. M. & Roby, Pamela. "Social Mobility, Equality and Education." *Social Policy,* May/June 1970b, pp. 38-40.

Miller, S. M., Reissman, F., & Seagull, A. A. "Poverty and Self-Indulgence: A Critique of the Non-Deferred Gratification Pattern." In L. S. Ferman, J. L. Kornbluh, & A. Haber (Eds.), *Poverty in America.* Revised Ed. Ann Arbor: University of Michigan Press, 1968. Pp. 416-432.

Miller, Walter B. "Lower Class Culture as a Generating Milieu of Gang Delinquency." *Journal of Social Issues,* 1958, Vol. XIV, No. 1, pp. 5-19.

Mishler, Elliot G., & Scotch, Norman A. "Sociocultural Factors in the Epidemiology of Schizophrenia: A Review." *Psychiatry,* 1963, Vol. 26, pp. 315-351.

Mishler, Elliot G., & Scotch, Norman A. "Sociological Factors in the Epidemiology of Schizophrenia." *International Journal of Psychiatry,* 1965, Vol. 1, pp. 258-305.

Mobilization For Youth, Inc. "A Proposal for the Prevention and Control of Juvenile Delinquency by Expanding Opportunities," New York, 1961.

Monahan, Thomas P. "Divorce by Occupational Level." *Marriage and Family Living,* 1955, Vol. 17, pp. 322-324.

Moynihan, Daniel P. "The Professionalization of Reform." *The Public Interest,* Fall 1965, No. 1, pp. 6-16.

Moynihan, Daniel P. *Maximum Feasible Misunderstanding.* New York: The Free Press, 1969.

Moynihan, Daniel P. *The Politics of a Guaranteed Income.* New York: Random House, 1973.

Murdock, George P. *Culture and Society.* Pittsburgh: University of Pittsburgh Press, 1969.

Myrdal, Gunnar. *An American Dilemma.* 2 Vols. New York: McGraw-Hill, 1964.

New York City, Temporary State Charter Revision Commission. Minutes of Meeting, November 22, 1972. Mahopac, N.Y.: O'Neill Reporting Co.

New York Times. "F. B. I. Crime Data Called Misleading by Sociologists," March 22, 1965.

New York Times. "Crime Statistics: A Numbers Game," February 4, 1968a.

New York Times. "Crime Statistics: Are They Reliable?" December 22, 1968b.

New York Times. "Transcript of Nixon's Address to Nation Outlining Proposals for Welfare Reform," August 9, 1969, p. 10.

New York Times. "'White Collar Strike' Forces Swedes to Question Welfare State's Future," February 26, 1971.

New York Times. "Swedes Debate the Impact of Welfare System On Their Freedom," November 12, 1972.

Offenbacher, Deborah I. "The Proper Study of Poverty: Empirical Versus Normative Perspectives." In Chaim I. Waxman, (Ed.), *Poverty: Power and Politics.* New York: Grosset & Dunlap, 1968. Pp. 37-63.

Offenbacher, Deborah I. *Cultures in Conflict.* Final Report to the U.S. Department of Health, Education, and Welfare, Office of Education, Bureau of Research, New York, 1969.

Offenbacher, Deborah I. & Poster, Constance H. *Social Problems and Social Policy.* New York: Appleton-Century-Crofts, 1970.

Ornati, Oscar. *Poverty Amid Affluence.* New York: The Twentieth Century Fund, 1966.

Park, Robert E. *Introduction to the Science of Sociology.* Second Edition. Chicago: University of Chicago Press, 1924.

Park, Robert E. "Human Ecology." In Ralph H. Turner, (Ed.), *Robert E. Park on Social Control and Collective Behavior.* Chicago: University of Chicago Press, 1967. Pp. 69-84.

Park, Robert E., & Ernest W. Burgess. *The City.* Chicago: University of Chicago Press, 1925.

Pasamanick, Benjamin (Ed.). *Epidemiology of Mental Disorder.* Washington, D. C.: American Association for the Advancement of Science, 1959.

Pavenstedt, Eleanor (Ed.). *The Drifters: Children of Disorganized Lower-Class Families.* Boston: Little, Brown, 1967.

Pfautz, Charles W. (Ed.). *Charles Booth on the City: Physical Patterns and Social Structure.* Chicago: University of Chicago Press, 1967.

Piven, Frances Fox, & Cloward, Richard A. *Regulating the Poor.* New York: Pantheon Books, 1971.

Polanyi, Karl. *The Great Transformation.* Boston: Beacon Press, 1957.

Poynter, J. R. *Society and Pauperism.* London: Routledge and Kegan Paul, 1969.

Rainwater, Lee. *And the Poor Get Children.* Chicago: Quadrangle Books, 1960.

Rainwater, Lee. "Working-Class Reality in Social Science: A Discussion." *Science and Society,* 1968, pp. 50-51.

Redbook Magazine: "A *Redbook* Dialogue: Robert Kennedy and Oscar Lewis," September 1967, pp. 74-75, 103-106.

Rein, Martin. "Social Science and the Elimination of Poverty." *Journal of the American Institute of Planners,* 1967, Vol. 33, No. 3.

Rein, Martin. *Social Policy.* New York: Random House, 1970.

Reiss, Albert J., Jr. *The Police and the Public.* New Haven: Yale University Press, 1971.

Reiss, Albert J., Jr., & Rhodes, Albert L. "The Distribution of Juvenile Delinquency in the Social Structure." *American Sociological Review,* 1961, Vol. 26, No. 5, pp. 720-732.

Rieff, Philip. *On Intellectuals.* Garden City: Doubleday Anchor Books, 1970.

Riessman, Catherine Kohler. "Birth Control, Culture, and the Poor." *American Journal of Orthopsychiatry,* 1968, Vol. 38, No. 4, pp. 693-699.

Riessman, Frank. *The Culturally Deprived Child.* New York: Harper and Row, 1962.

Riessman, Frank. "Self-Help Among the Poor." *Trans-Action,* Sept./Oct. 1965, Vol. 2, pp. 32-37.

Riessman, Frank. "The Myth of Saul Alinsky." *Dissent,* July-August, 1967, pp. 469-478.

Riessman, Frank, Cohen, Jerome, & Pearl, Arthur, (Eds.).*Mental Health of the Poor.* New York: The Free Press, 1964.

Roach, Jack L. "Social Scientific Knowledge and Social Application: An Essay Review." *Social Work,* October 1967, Vol. 12, pp. 108-11.

Roach, Jack L., & Gursslin, Orville R. "An Evaluation of the Concept, 'Culture of Poverty.' " *Social Forces,* 1967, Vol. 45, No. 3, pp. 383-392.

Robison, Sophia M. "A Critical View of the Uniform Crime Reports." *Michigan Law Review,* 1966, Vol. LXIV, No. 6, pp. 1031-1054.

Rodman, Hyman. "The Lower Class Value Stretch." *Social Forces,* 1963, Vol. 42, pp. 205-215.

Rodman, Hyman. "Illegitimacy in the Caribbean Social Structure: A Review." *American Sociological Review,* 1966, Vol. 31, pp. 673-683.

Rodman, Hyman. "Controversies About Lower-Class Culture: Delinquency and Illegitimacy." *Canadian Review of Sociology and Anthropology,* 1969, Vol. 5, No. 4, pp. 254-262.

Rodman, Hyman. *Lower-Class Families: The Culture of Poverty in Negro Trinidad.* New York: Oxford University Press, 1971.

Rodman, Hyman, & Grams, Paul. "Juvenile Delinquency and the Family: A Review and Discussion." *Task Force Report: Juvenile Delinquency and Youth Crime.* Washington, D.C.: United States Government Printing Office, 1967, pp. 188-221.

Rokeach, Milton & Parker, Seymour. "Values as Social Indicators of Poverty and Race Relations in America." *The Annals*, March 1970, Vol. 388, pp. 87-111.

Roman, Paul M., & Trice, M. Harrison. *Schizophrenia and the Poor.* Ithaca: New York State School of Industrial and Labor Relations, Cornell University, 1967.

Rosen, Bernard C. "The Achievement Syndrome: A Psychocultural Dimension of Social Stratification." *American Sociological Review,* 1956, Vol. 21, pp. 203-211.

Rosen, Bernard C. "Race, Ethnicity, and the Achievement Syndrome." *American Sociological Review*, 1959, pp. 47-60.

Rosenberg, Bernard, Gerver, Israel, & Howton, F. William (Eds.). *Mass Society in Crisis.* New York: Macmillan, 1964.

Rosenberg, Bernard & Silverstein, Harry. *The Varieties of Delinquent Experience.* Waltham, Mass.: Blaisdell, 1969.

Ross, Arthur M., & Hill, Herbert, (Eds.). *Employment, Race and Poverty.* New York: Harcourt, Brace and World, 1967.

Roszak, Theodore. *The Making of a Counter Culture.* Garden City: Doubleday Anchor Books, 1969.

Rubin, Lillian B. "Maximum Feasible Participation: The Origins, Implications and Present Status." *Poverty and Human Resources Abstracts,* Nov./Dec. 1967, Vol. 2, pp. 5-18.

Runciman, W. G. *Relative Deprivation and Social Justice.* Berkeley: University of California Press, 1966.

Ryan, William. *Blaming the Victim.* New York: Pantheon Books, 1971.

Scase, Richard (Ed.). *Readings in the Swedish Class Structure.* Oxford and New York: Pergamon Press, 1976.

Seeley, John R., Sim, R. Alexander & Loosley, Elizabeth W. *Crestwood Heights: A Study of the Culture of Suburban Life.* New York: Wiley Science Editions, 1963.

Sexton, Patricia Cayo. *Education and Income.* New York: The Viking Press, 1961.

Shils, Edward. "The Intellectual and the Powers: Some Perspectives for Comparative Analysis." In P. Rieff (Ed.), *On Intellectuals.* Garden City: Doubleday Anchor Books, 1970. Pp. 27-51.

Shostak, Arthur B., & Gomberg, William (Eds.). *New Perspectives on Poverty.* Englewood Cliffs: Prentice Hall, 1965.

Smith, Adam. *An Inquiry into the Nature and Causes of the Wealth of Nations*. New York: Modern Library, 1937.

Spencer, Herbert. *The Study of Sociology*. Ann Arbor: University of Michigan Press, 1961.

Srole, Leo, Langner, Thomas S., Michael, Stanley T., Kirkpatrick, Price, Opler, Marvin K., Rennie, Thomas A. C. *Mental Health in the Metropolis: The Midtown Manhattan Study*. New York: McGraw Hill, 1962.

Steiner, Gilbert Y. *Social Insecurity: The Politics of Welfare. Chicago:* Rand McNally, 1966.

Steiner, Gilbert Y. *The State of Welfare*. Washington, D.C.: The Brookings Institution, 1971.

Sumner, William Graham. *Folkways*. New York: Dover Publications, 1959.

Sundquist, James L. (Ed.). *On Fighting Poverty*. New York: Basic Books, 1969.

Sutherland, Edwin H. *White Collar Crime*. New York: Holt, Rinehart and Winston, 1949.

Sutherland, Edwin H. "White Collar Criminality." *American Sociological Review,* 1940, Vol. 5, No. 1, pp. 1-12.

Suttles, Gerald D. *The Social Order of the Slum*. Chicago: University of Chicago Press, 1968.

Szasz, Thomas S. *Ideology and Insanity*. Garden City: Doubleday Anchor Books, 1970.

Talmon, Yonina. *Family and Community in the Kibbutz*. Cambridge: Harvard University Press, 1972.

TenBroek, Jacobus, & Matson, Floyd W. *Hope Deferred: Public Welfare and the Blind*. Berkeley: University of California Press, 1959.

Thomas, W. I. "The Individualization of Behavior." In Morris Janowitz, (Ed.), *W. I. Thomas on Social Organization and Social Personality*. Chicago: University of Chicago Press, 1966. Pp. 231-253.

Thomas, W. I. *The Unadjusted Girl*. New York: Harper Torchbooks, 1969.

Thrasher, Frederick M. *The Gang*. Abridged Edition. Chicago: University of Chicago Press, 1963.

Time Magazine. "Crime: Meaningless Statistics?" August 19, 1966.

Time Magazine. "Race and Ability," Sept. 29, 1967.

Titmuss, Richard M. *Commitment to Welfare*. New York: Pantheon Books, 1968.

Titmuss, Richard M. *Social Policy*. New York: Pantheon Books, 1974.

Toby, Jackson. "Orientation to Education as a Factor in the School Maladjustment of Lower-Class Children." *Social Forces,* 1957, Vol. 35, pp. 259-266.

Toby, Jackson. "The Socialization and Control of Deviant Motivation." In D. Glaser (Ed.), *Handbook of Criminology*. Chicago: Rand McNally, 1974. Pp. 85-100.

Townsend, Joseph. *A Dissertation on the Poor Laws: By a Well-Wisher to Mankind,* 1786. Reprinted with a Foreword by Ashley Montagu and an Afterword by Mark Neuman. Berkeley: University of California Press, 1971.

Townsend, Peter (Ed.). *The Concept of Poverty.* New York: American Elsevier, 1970. Pp. 1-45.

Townsend, Peter. "Measures and Explanations of Poverty in High Income and Low Income Countries: The Problems of Operationalizing the Concepts of Development, Class and Poverty." In Peter Townsend (Ed.), *The Concept of Poverty.* New York: American Elsevier, 1970. Pp. 1-45.

Tumin, Melvin M. (Ed.). *Readings on Social Stratification.* Englewood Cliffs: Prentice Hall, 1970.

Turner, R. Jay, & Wagenfeld, Morton O. "Occupational Mobility and Schizophrenia." *American Sociological Review,* 1967, Vol. 32, pp. 104-113.

United States Government. *Economic Report to the President, 1964.* Washington, D. C.: United Stated Government Printing Office, 1964.

United States Government. *Task Force Report. Juvenile Delinquency and Youth Crime.* Washington, D. C.: United States Government Printing Office, 1967.

United States Government. United States Commission on Civil Rights: *Racial Isolation in the Public Schoools.* Washington, D. C.: United States Government Printing Office, 1967, Vol. 1.

United States Government. United States Department of Health, Education and Welfare. "Welfare Myths Versus Facts." Washington, D.C.: United States Government Printing Office, 1971.

United States Government. United States Senate. *Federal Role in Urban Affairs,* Part 13. Washington, D.C.: United States Government Printing Office, 1967.

United States Government. United States Supreme Court. *Shapiro v. Thompson,* 89 S.Ct. 1322 (1969).

United States Government. United States Supreme Court. *San Antonio Independent School District v. Rodrigues,* 93 S.Ct. 1278 (1973).

United States Government. United States Supreme Court. *DeFunis v. Odegaard,* 94 S.Ct. (1974).

Valentine, Charles A. *Culture and Poverty.* Chicago: University of Chicago Press, 1968.

Wallace, Samuel E. *Skid Row as a Way of Life.* New York: Harper Torchbooks, 1968.

Walter, E. V. "The Spirit of Poverty," 1970, mimeographed.

Warner, W. Lloyd. *Yankee City*. Abridged Edition. New Haven: Yale University Press, 1963.

Warner, W. Lloyd, Bunker, Bulford H., & Adams, Walter A. *Color and Human Nature*. New York: Harper Torchbooks, 1969.

Wasserman, Miriam. *The School Fix, N. Y. C., U. S. A*. New York: Outerbridge and Dienstfrey, 1970.

Waxman, Chaim I. "Culture, Poverty and Ideology." In I. Deborah Offenbacher & Constance H. Poster, (Eds.), *Social Problems and Social Policy*. New York: Appleton-Century-Crofts, 1970. Pp. 55-64.

Waxman, Chaim I. (Ed.) *Poverty: Power and Politics*. New York: Grosset & Dunlap, 1968.

Webb, Sydney, & Webb, Beatrice. *English Poor Law History, Part I, The Old Poor Law*. Reprinted with a New Introduction by W. A. Robson. Hamden, Conn.: Archon Books, 1963.

Weber, Max. *The Protestant Ethic and the Spirit of Capitalism*, Translated by Talcott Parsons. New York: Charles Scribner's Sons, 1958.

Weber, Max. *Economy and Society,* 3 Vols. Edited by Guenther Roth and Claus Wittich. New York: Bedminister Press, 1968.

Wedderburn, Dorothy (Ed.). *Poverty, Inequality and Class Structure*. London: Cambridge University Press, 1974.

Weinraub, Bernard. "Swedish Socialists Lose to Coalition After 44-year Rule." *New York Times,* September 20, 1976.

Wilcox, Preston. "Social Policy and White Racism." *Social Policy,* May/June, 1970, pp. 41-46.

Wilensky, Harold L. "The Welfare Mess." *Transaction/SOCIETY,* May/June 1976, Vol. 13, No. 4, pp. 12-16, 64.

Wolfgang, Marvin E. "Uniform Crime Reporting: A Critical Reappraisal." *University of Pennsylvania Law Review,* 1963, Vol. III, No. 9, pp. 708-738.

Woodroofe, Kathleen. *From Charity to Social Work*. Toronto: University of Toronto Press, 1966.

Yancey, William L. "The Culture of Poverty: Not So Much Parsimony." 1965, mimeographed.

Zorbaugh, Harvey W. *The Gold Coast and the Slum*. Chicago: University of Chicago Press, 1929.

Name Index

Subject Index